Talk Sporty
to Me

Thinking Outside
the Box Scores

Jen Mueller

Norsemen Books

Norsemen Books and Talk Sporty to Me are registered trademarks

Print Edition ISBN: 978-0-9937968-2-1
eBook Edition ISBN: 978-0-9937968-3-8

Cover design by Gina O'Daniel, O'Daniel Designs
Printed in the United States of America
Published by Norsemen Books

Talk Sporty to Me
Bothell, WA
www.TalkSportyToMe.com

*ATTENTION CORPORATIONS, UNIVERSITIES, COLLEGES AND PROFESSIONAL ORGANIZATIONS: Quantity discounts are available on bulk purchases of this book for educational, gift purposes, or as premiums for increasing memberships. Special book covers or book excerpts can be created to fit specific needs. For more information, please contact Norsemen Books: info@norsemenbooks.com or 1-206-734-4950

Praise for Jen Mueller and Talk Sporty to Me

Because of Jen's vast sports knowledge, having covered many college and professional sports teams, she has learned and understands the many valuable tools and principles gained from sports. Jen has gone a step further, taking these same tools and principles and applied them to the business and corporate world. Jen has helped many companies benefit by making corporate America understand how the two are similar for success.

Warren Moon
Hall of Fame Quarterback

It's just a short statement, as obvious as the overly large, several-times broken nose on my face. And Jen captured perfectly the gist of her interesting and relevant book Talk Sporty to Me. 'Everyone is a fan of something.' Simple. Direct. It can be food, or furniture. Cars or cats, or SPORTS! And Jen does a superb job of breaking down exactly why sports chat works in virtually any setting, for anybody.

Steve Raible
Voice of the Seattle Seahawks

A must read! Jen artfully showcases how talking sports is an equalizer, a common denominator that thoroughly understood can propel your ability to navigate conversation to your benefit and career success.

Amy Sprangers
Vice President Corporate Partnerships & Suites,
Seattle Seahawks

Jen is a terrific broadcaster and an enthusiastic "people connector". In her newest book, Talk Sporty to Me: Thinking Outside the Box Scores, the tangible, real-life strategies for how to use sports in making connections and establishing relationships hit the mark.

Frances Traisman
Vice President Sales, Seattle Mariners

Finally, the ultimate playbook for learning the winning edge in the workplace! Jen Mueller offers brilliant insights into concepts that will give you a competitive advantage in your career advancement. Jen clearly demonstrates how small talk and sports talk isn't a waste of time but a proven strategy to improve communication skills, strengthen relationships and build a team. This is a fun and engaging must read for college students or any fan looking for more reasons to talk about their favorite team.

Chris Morris
Director of Campus Recreation,
Florida State University

Acknowledgements

"Fight like hell until someone listens."

That was the advice from John Nordstrom as I prepared to release this book. I was frustrated that no one else could see my vision and wondered if I could make the difference in peoples' lives that I'd hoped. The jury is still out on that one, but John has certainly made a difference to me. I cannot thank him enough for his willingness to talk to me for this book and for his graciousness in always finding a minute to talk and share business insights.

The same thing could be said of Tom Kardashian. Thank you for that initial phone call and your consistent encouragement.

Sometimes I pinch myself just to make sure it isn't all just a wonderful dream. I am truly blessed to be where I am in my career and have the opportunity to work with and learn from such incredible people. The list includes: Pete Carroll, John Schneider and the entire Seattle Seahawks organization, the Seattle Mariners, and my colleagues at ROOT SPORTS.

To all of the news directors, executive producers, reporters, editors and anchors I've worked with throughout the years, thank you. I learned so much from each one of you and wouldn't trade the challenges of a television career for anything.

To the athletes and coaches I work with, it's an honor to tell your stories and have a front row seat for all your success.

To my former teachers, family and friends, yes, I know "I talk too much." It's been quite useful in my career, but thank you for putting up with it when it was just a nuisance.

Thank you to my girlfriends who keep me sane and are quick to offer a glass of wine when I need a break from the testosterone-filled locker rooms.

Thank you doesn't begin to express my appreciation or gratitude toward my family, especially Josh, Jessica and Paul. My schedule revolves around sports, but you are always in my heart.

Finally to mom and dad, thank you for believing in me. I love you.

"For I know the plans I have for you," declares the Lord, "plans to prosper you and not to harm you, plans to give you hope and a future." Jeremiah 29:11

Table of Contents

Introduction   9

Chapter 1 –Winning Strategies   15

Chapter 2 –Speak My Language   29

Chapter 3 –Small Talk & Productivity   51

Chapter 4 – Why Sports?   71

Chapter 5 – Leveraging Sports Fandom   87

Chapter 6 –Business Building Strategies   103

Chapter 7– Conversation Game Plan   119

Chapter 8–Guaranteed Success   139

What Do I Say If...?   151

Quick Guide to Networking with Sports   161

Epilogue   167

About the Author   171

"Every week is a championship opportunity"
Seattle Seahawks

Introduction

INTRODUCTION

"Little things make the big things happen."

John Wooden

"It's all a matter of perspective."

That's what the tour guide said as we approached the Parthenon in Athens, Greece. We had hiked to the top of the acropolis and were staring in amazement at the historic structure. The guide invited us to step closer and inspect the columns.

"You should notice," she said, "that none of them are straight."

It didn't seem possible. I had taken pictures of the Parthenon from a vantage point in the city and even among the ruins, every column looked perfectly straight. But as I stood there examining the architecture, I realized she was right. Each column was slightly off to give it the illusion of being perfectly straight from a distance. The variations were something that could only be noticed by standing directly in front of each one.

Changing my perspective gave me an entirely new appreciation for the Parthenon. Standing at a distance caused the details to go unnoticed and standing too close minimized the true scale of the architects' accomplishments.

It's all a matter of perspective...

The statement is true in most instances of business, relationships and life. Change your perspective and you'll likely notice something new and perhaps unexpected.

The goal of this book is to change your perspective on how you view sports and sports fandom. As a life-long sports fan and a veteran sports broadcaster, I understand how to view sports in terms of wins and losses, statistics and trends. As a business owner, I understand how sports can be a valuable business tool; one that bridges communications gaps, opens doors to influential people and gives me an advantage in every conversation.

I know from more than 15 years in sports broadcasting that most fans view sports primarily in terms of wins and losses. They miss the bigger perspective. It's like looking at a dartboard and focusing solely on the center bull's eye without realizing there are a number of rings that expand out from the center of the target. There's nothing wrong with paying attention to wins and losses, but if it's the only thing you focus on you're missing the bigger picture.

If you're a non-sports fan looking at the big picture but unable to make sense of it, changing your perspective could help. Understanding the business value of a sports conversation can help you prioritize the information you need and lead to an interest level that works for you.

Either way, whether you're already a sports fan or not sure what the fuss is about, this book is for you. Sports is the language of business. Like it or not, a 30-second sports conversation can open more doors and connect you with a larger audience than your resume. Talent and skill are important, but the ability to communicate and connect with others plays a significant role in your success. The greatest ideas and the best inventions will go unnoticed and unused if you can't tell the world – or worse – no one listens when you try.

This book demonstrates how sports conversations and sports fandom will get you noticed, connected and communicating more effectively. Add that up and you're looking at more opportunities and greater successes.

It seems hard to believe that sports can do all of those things, but I promise it can.

It's all a matter of perspective.

I invite you to change yours and gain a new appreciation of how you can put sports fandom to work for you.

"Talent and skill are important, but the ability to communicate and connect with others plays a significant role in your success."

Chapter 1 – Winning Strategies

"You can win in any business situation by communicating more effectively, and your strategy should start with sports conversations."

February 2, 2014.

The clock ticked down to zero. Green and blue confetti shot from the rafters of MetLife Stadium in New Jersey and covered the field. The Seattle Seahawks had just beaten the Denver Broncos 43–8 in Super Bowl XLVIII. Moments after the trophy presentation on the field, Seahawks head coach Pete Carroll addressed the media and said this:

"I think as we have seen in the past, sometimes games go, and sometimes it can be kind of like an avalanche. The scores start happening. Field position just tilts and everything goes your way. We were really ready. We were really ready for the opportunities."

I was on the sidelines for that game working on the Seahawks' radio broadcast and that's exactly what it felt like. An avalanche. You could feel the momentum building. You could see the game plan come together. You could see the results of a season of hard work. Pete's description of the game was certainly an accurate one, but as he described the win and the feeling inside the organization, I thought back to another organization that described its success in much the same way,

"It was like a tidal wave. We could feel the momentum building. By the time everyone else realized what was happening it was too late. We crushed the competition and they couldn't catch up."

That's how John Nordstrom explained the success and growth of Nordstrom department stores in the 1970s. It was early in 2011, and he and I were sitting in the cafeteria at the Seahawks training facility. John, the former owner of the Seahawks, patiently answered my questions about how he grew Nordstrom from a local family-owned store to a nationally recognized brand. I was particularly interested in how he implemented the store's well-known customer service policy. He recounted his months of research, the actual implementation process and finally the tidal wave of results.

I took pages of notes during that lunch, trying to capture every detail and facet of Nordstrom's success. As I poured over my notes later that afternoon, I realized there were a number of factors that led to John's success in business, but I could sum them up in two statements:

1. John differentiated Nordstrom from the competition by asking the question, "How can we take advantage of our competitors?"

2. After he determined the strategy, he had a simple plan for implementation.

Here's what happened:

John and the incoming leadership at Nordstrom spent six months scouting the competition, looking for opportunities to win customers. At the end of that time, the leadership group met and determined there were three areas they couldn't stand out: buildings, merchandise and price. As John explained to me, they were not interested in building bigger, more grandiose buildings. Nor were they going to be able to offer merchandise that differed greatly enough from the competition to draw customers on a consistent basis. And when it comes to price, it's essentially a no-win situation.

This all helped highlight their key opportunity for success – customer service. Decades later John still spoke of the joy he felt in seeing how poorly this was carried out in other stores as he witnessed their customer service in action.

"I remember walking into a prominent high-fashion store in Beverly Hills," John said. "There was a man walking through the men's department with a stack of shirts and a couple of ties. He was just wandering around looking for some assistance. One sales person saw him and took off to the back of the store. Two more sales clerks were talking to each other at the counter, but neither offered to help. As the man is standing there, the guy vacuuming the department asked him to move out of the way.

"I almost died laughing," John recalled smiling. "It was a defining moment."

It's why he determined Nordstrom could take advantage of its competitors by putting the customers first and placing a heavy emphasis on customer service. That's what he set about doing shortly after taking the reins in 1968.

When it came to implementing the strategy, John didn't issue a directive or mandate specific procedures. He didn't order employees to be better. Instead, he made a suggestion.

"Our overall goal was to satisfy a customer's shopping wants," John said. "So I suggested [to the employees] that when it came to the customers, our number one goal could be to provide outstanding customer service. And I said, 'Let us know if you agree with that. If so, let's go with it.'"

The Nordstrom employees agreed and bought in. But even then, they weren't issued a list of rules to follow. So how did they reach the goal?

Ask John this question and he'll hold up his hand, nearly pinch his thumb and index finger together and squint through the small sliver of space between them. Then he'll say, "by getting this much better."

"We asked them to improve customer service a little bit at a time because everyone thinks they can improve a little bit," John explained.

John helped create a culture of "buy-in" at Nordstrom and cultivated a willingness to get a little better every day. It was reflected in their employee handbook, which for years was a half sheet of paper containing just six sentences.

Near the top of the page it reads: "Our number one goal is to provide **outstanding customer service.**"

Two sentences later it says: "**Use your good judgment in all situations.**"

That simple, straightforward message combined with the desire to get a little better has led to extraordinary efforts to assist customers.

"Picture this," John said. "You're on a business trip. You're scheduled to give a presentation at 8 o'clock in the morning. You arrive at your hotel late the night before only to discover you forgot to pack your dress shoes. What do you do? The stores are already closed for the night and they won't be open in time for you to make a purchase in the morning."

If you're a loyal Nordstrom customer or a customer familiar with Nordstrom's customer service goal you might call the emergency number at the local Nordstrom store and see if there's anything they can do.

According to John, this has happened more than once. In one instance, a customer called at about 11 o'clock in the evening and ended up speaking to the cleaning manager on duty. After hearing the situation the cleaning manager made arrangements to meet the customer at the receiving door. He ushered him into the back of the store and located the boxes of men's dress shoes. "I don't know anything about dress shoes," the cleaning manager said, "but we'll make sure you find the pair you need." And they did.

John points to a combination of the customer service focus and the employee buy-in as the reason he still receives emails from customers around the country who want to share their experiences about the above-and-beyond efforts of a Nordstrom employee.

There were plenty of people who initially thought his approach was unconventional and questioned its effectiveness.

"Now they know it works like crazy," John said.

It took a little time, but his approach more than moved the meter. In 1971 Nordstrom sales were about $80 million. In 1980, nearly a decade after the customer service strategy was implemented, sales topped $407 million. The company continues to grow and customers consistently rate Nordstrom higher than any other department store chain according to the American Customer Satisfaction Index – including the last seven straight years.

The similarity between the verbiage Pete Carroll used in talking about the Super Bowl so closely matched the way I heard John talk about his success, that I couldn't help make the comparison.

Pete uses a simple, straightforward philosophy of "Always Compete." (His book Win Forever outlines how he arrived at his approach and his central theme of competition.) I watched from the sidelines as Pete implemented this strategy in 2010 in his first season as the Seahawks head coach. I continued to watch as the players bought in and truly understood the significance of it during the Super Bowl run in 2013.

The message that stood out to me the most that season (and continues to impress me now) is: "Every game is a championship opportunity." The Seahawks don't treat one game more importantly than another because every win is important. Every practice and every meeting leading up to each game is a chance to get a little better and prepare to take advantage of the opponent on game day.

To me, it wasn't hard to draw a connection between Pete and John. They are two successful men who understand how to innovate, motivate and run successful teams – and I'd seen them interact with each other hundreds of times on the football field.

As the former owner of the Seahawks, John regularly attends practices and accompanies the team on road trips throughout the season. John is as quick to talk football as he is business, and my favorite days at practice are ones that I spend talking to John. What starts as a comment about the chemistry of the defense could easily turn into a business lesson on cultivating teamwork in an office.

The transition between football and business happens so smoothly with John that it's easy to forget the talking point that started the conversation: football.

In case you forgot, it's also the topic that started this chapter.

The connection between Nordstrom department stores and the Seattle Seahawks shows how a winning strategy can start with a simple goal that leads to big results. It also illustrates how closely sports and business can be aligned.

If you're starting to think of the sports metaphors that apply to your workplace, like "let's go knock this out of the park" stop. That's not where this is going.

What do I want you to notice? The conversation about the Seahawks' win against the Denver Broncos could be all about the numbers: the final score, the quarterback ratings, the total yards allowed, touchdowns scored, etc. That's the way most fans talk about the game with me. Or the conversation could be one relating to Pete's approach to practice, preparation and execution, which happens to be similar to conversations that have played out in all types of work environments, including Nordstrom department stores.

Sports conversations can be more than stats, final scores and Xs and Os. Sports conversations can lead to bigger conversations.

Now it's time to look at how Pete and John's approaches apply to you:

1. What is going to separate you from the competition?

2. What is your simple implementation strategy?

There are plenty of answers to those questions, but for the purposes of this book and the chapters that follow, I'm going to offer this suggestion:

You can win in any business situation by communicating more effectively, and your strategy should start with sports conversations.

Speak sports. Talk business.

This doesn't mean that you have to become a raging sports fan or a sports expert. It doesn't mean that the only thing you ever talk about is sports. What it means is this: sports is the easiest way to gain a foothold in a conversation. It's one of the most effective ways at initiating a connection and building a relationship. You'll see how this plays out in the coming chapters.

Business isn't just about who you know, it's about the relationships you have with the people you know. Money doesn't change hands if there isn't a relationship in place and relationships don't happen without communication.

Conversations are vital in business and simply having more of them doesn't necessarily improve communication. Developing a winning conversation strategy is similar to Nordstrom developing a winning customer service strategy. Neither requires a large output of resources, both focus on meeting individual needs and both can lead to financial rewards.

Successful people develop winning strategies.

With that in mind, let's get to work.

Chapter Recap

Simple, straightforward philosophies led to big results for John Nordstrom and Pete Carroll. Get the results you're looking for by remembering these key takeaways:

Big results start as small commitments

Improve communication skills

Generate connections between sports and business

"Daily interactions are the lifeblood of any business. The way people relate and communicate with each other has a direct impact on relationships and productivity. When communication styles miss the mark, money is left on the table.

Chapter 2 – Speak My Language

"Just because you're speaking the same language doesn't mean you're actually speaking the same language."

Cuban-born slugger Kendrys Morales spent the 2013 Major League Baseball season with the Seattle Mariners. Even after six big league seasons in the United States, speaking English didn't come easy for Kendrys. Spanish was his preferred language and starting in Spring Training that year I made it a point to dust off what I'd learned in five years of Spanish classes and use it in conversation with Kendrys.

Every day that season I walked into the clubhouse and spoke a couple sentences to Kendrys in Spanish. He would answer in English. It was a way for us to meet in the middle and get more comfortable speaking the other person's language. A few months into the season I asked Kendrys if he would be comfortable doing what we call a "walk-off" interview in English. Those are the interviews that happen on the field immediately after the game with a player who made a significant contribution in the win. He agreed, if I asked the questions in Spanish.

A few weeks later Kendrys hit a three-run homer that helped power the Mariners to a win. It was the first of two walk-off interviews we did that season. After both, I heard from fans who weren't happy that I asked the questions in Spanish (which I translated for the entire audience). When they asked why I did it I explained that I wanted to speak in a way he could understand.

Kendrys could answer a question in English, but he wanted to make sure that he fully understood the question first. The best way for me to help with that was to ask the question in his native language. Hearing and understanding his own language helped give him the confidence to speak in mine.

International travelers will likely relate to this story. Attempting to speak the language of the country you're visiting is often seen as a gesture of respect and goodwill. You'll get a lot further with the locals when you try to communicate in a way that's familiar to them.

The same could be said with every interaction we have during the course of the day. You don't have to travel to a foreign country to run into a communication barrier. It happens all the time whether you're aware of it or not. Just because you're speaking the same language doesn't mean you're actually speaking the same language.

- Think about the colleague who takes 10 minutes to explain a problem that could have been outlined in two minutes. At what point do you start to tune out?

- What about the co-worker that typically engages in short, abrupt conversations that make you wonder if he's mad at you?

- Then there's the friend that uses way too many details when describing her weekend on Monday mornings. Does your mind start to wander and think about other things during that conversation? Does it ever make you question whether she approaches conversations with key clients in the same way?

On the surface none of those scenarios seem so bad, but think a little harder.

- Have you missed important details in a meeting, causing you to go back and have another conversation, because of a long-winded explanation?

- Have you ever fretted and worried about a perceived "rude" colleague and lost concentration on the task at hand?

- Have you ever found yourself avoiding colleagues who talk too much?

If you're still wondering, "What's the big deal?" realize that daily interactions are the lifeblood of any business. The way people relate and communicate with each other has a direct impact on relationships and productivity. When communication styles miss the mark, money is left on the table.

In other words, conversations throughout the day impact the bottom line.

As a sports broadcaster I am very aware of the importance of daily conversations and interactions. My ability to talk to athletes directly impacts my relationships with them, which in turn affects the quality of the interviews I get, increases the satisfaction of the fans at home and reinforces my value on the broadcast team. It's why I continue to get a paycheck.

I know that I was born to talk. Every teacher I ever had in grade school and middle school wrote the same comment on my report card: "Jennifer is a good student, but she talks too much." I joke now that it was just practice for my career. Even though some of us are more comfortable talking to other people, we can all benefit from having a few guidelines in place. These are the same guidelines I follow every day with coaches, players, front office staff, executives and my own business contacts.

Here are the three most important things to understand in every conversation:

1. Topic

2. Timing

3. Productivity

Topic

Let's start with the basic idea of a conversation as defined by Webster's dictionary: an oral exchange of sentiments, observations, opinions or ideas.

On the surface that seems about right, but it does leave out a few important details. For example, it doesn't offer much guidance in the way of what we should be talking about or how long a good conversation should last. Trust me, opinions vary depending on whom you ask. Many times men tend to think one way and women the other.

I'm sure you're not surprised to know that men and women approach conversations differently, but understanding how they differ will shed a lot of light on your daily interactions.[1]

According to renowned linguist Deborah Tannen, men and women have two separate agendas in any given conversation. In general, men in a conversation are **seeking information** while women are **looking for intimacy and connection**. Those conversation

---

[1] I've been told categorizing conversation differences between men and women could be perceived as sexist or offensive. That's certainly not my intent and it's not the intent of the scientific research done on the subject. There is no right or wrong way to communicate; there are just more effective ways than others to get your point across. Understanding the different factors at play can help you become a more effective communicator overall.

objectives are at completely opposite ends of the spectrum and lead to different conversation topics.

This helps to explain how I was able to strike up a conversation with complete strangers while in line for a porta potty prior to running a marathon. It doesn't matter whom I'm talking to as long as I'm talking to someone. (I never said the comments of "talks too much" were unwarranted.) It also helps to explain my tendency to share every detail of my day with my spouse. The more details I share the stronger I think the connection becomes and the better I feel about the relationship. It's also why I enjoy my job in broadcasting so much. When people talk to me I feel good. It's as simple as that.

The topic of my conversations could be anything at all. I could literally find something to talk about for everything. Even if I was telling you how much I didn't know about it. That is not how most men approach conversation topics.

The men I work with (i.e. athletes and coaches) and often times my spouse, aren't interested in the minutiae of my day because they're looking for what they perceive to be "real" information. They want hard core facts, numbers and deadlines. It's what they would prefer to talk about most of the time and it seems like a productive way to approach business deals...unless it's not what the client wants to talk about.

I watched an interesting conversation play out while tagging along on a sales call a couple years ago. The buyer was a woman. The sales person was a man. He kept hammering the numbers while she kept asking him to paint a picture of what the benefits looked like. He thought the biggest selling point was the deal he could give her in dollars. She didn't care as much about the dollars. She had the money to spend and wanted to understand how buying advertising in a television show would give her more visibility with customers.

We walked out of the meeting and Sam, the sales person, looked at me and said. "Can you believe it? Some women just don't understand good numbers." I looked at him and said. "She didn't care about the numbers. You didn't give her what she really wanted. If you did she would have bought."

Sam was stunned and so was I. Neither person was speaking the same language during that sales call. Not only did Sam not recognize that, but he also didn't make an effort to speak the buyer's language. The end result? He lost a potential client. This is not to say that women don't understand numbers or can't talk about them. It's merely an example and a reminder that sometimes numbers don't just sell themselves.

I'm not in sales meetings as often as I am on a football or baseball field for post-game interviews, but the same dynamic comes into play. In some ways I'm a sales person during those interviews because I am trying to get a player to buy-in to telling me the story of the game.

I had a conversation with Mariners infielder Willie Bloomquist at Spring Training in 2013. During that talk he very frankly said, "You know the question I hate most after games? The one that starts with 'How did you feel?' Why do people ask that and why does it matter how I felt? Ask me about the game."

A couple months into the season, Willie hit a home run for the first time in three seasons. I approached him after the game for a walk-off interview. Instead of asking, "How did it feel?" I took this approach, "We saw you pull the ball on that home run, something we don't see often. What were you looking for in that at bat?"

His answer was funny, gracious and informative. Catering the question to his conversation needs led to the best possible outcome. He gave a great answer that the fans enjoyed and I felt good about a job well done, which is part of feeling connected to the people around you.

So, if men and women differ in the subject matter they prefer to talk about, it helps to explain the amount of time each usually spends talking.

Timing

I love posing this question to large groups during my corporate training sessions: "How long does the perfect conversation last?"

Usually I ask the women to go first, and I encourage them to think outside of the workplace setting. Picture an afternoon with girlfriends and nothing else on the schedule. Throw in some wine if that helps, and tell me how long that conversation lasts. Nearly every single time I have asked the question the women in the audience have said between two and three hours. At which point the mouth of every man in the audience drops open and hits the floor.

I pose the same question to the men, but with a slightly difference emphasis:

"Given your druthers, how long does the perfect conversation last?"

Men are perfectly capable of talking for long periods of time, but I want to know what a conversation looks like in their perfect world. If I am trying to make them feel most comfortable, how long does that conversation last? More than 95 percent of the time the answer is between five and 10 minutes – a revelation that usually shocks the women in the room.

At this point, I like to remind everyone in the audience that there is no right or wrong answer, but clearly there is a big difference between two hours and five minutes. That gap can become a huge communication barrier.

If I, as a woman, am predisposed to thinking that longer conversations are better, I probably won't think twice about a conversation that lasts 15 minutes. But what happens if I'm talking to a male colleague who approaches conversations with the "less is more" mindset? Five minutes into that conversation he will mentally move on to other things and there's a good chance that anything I say after those first five minutes goes unheard.

My producer reminded me that "less is more" during the 2014 Mariners season. My daily responsibilities included conducting a quick one-on-one interview with manager Lloyd McClendon. My producer approached me one day when I got to the ballpark and said, "Hey Jen, we've noticed your questions in the interviews are getting a little long. Don't forget McClendon seems to respond better to shorter, more direct questions." I didn't need any further explanation. I knew the research behind it. Asking shorter, more direct questions wasn't my preferred style in those situations, but it didn't matter because it was his. When I adapted my approach, I got more out of those interviews.

Understanding this dynamic has huge impacts on the way we talk in business.

The same thing happens in emails. I worked with a colleague, Jill, whose job included sending out comprehensive and detailed emails on a weekly basis. She was great at keeping everyone on the same page, but she wished everyone would read the emails she sent. Several times a week I heard her say, "It's in the email I sent." Guess who she was saying that to? A handful of men in the office.

Jill isn't the only woman dealing with this dynamic at work. I hear stories similar to this every time I speak to an audience. Jill is doing exactly what she's supposed to in sending out the emails, but she's just running up against the five-minute window. In email form that translates to about a paragraph and a few bullet points. It's not just the amount of time it takes to read it, but also the way the information is presented and laid out. You can include all the details and information you want, but if men are looking for shorter interactions your message will be better received if you deliver it in quick exchanges.

My job covering the Seattle Mariners requires regular interaction with members of their front office staff. Rarely will I send an email that is longer than five one-sentence bullet points. It's usually closer to three sentences long because I know they don't have time to sort through paragraphs of details, ideas and explanations.

I'm going to hit the pause button for just a second and say that this is not a hard and fast rule that only applies to men. My communication preference at work has changed over the years. Sure I can talk for two hours to a girlfriend, but when I'm trying to get things done, I want short conversations and short emails. Many women in the corporate world feel this way, especially if they have worked in a male dominated environment for a significant period of time. These are general guidelines to help you formulate more effective communication strategies and understand where your colleagues might be coming from.

We've already seen that long conversations or emails can cause a male colleague to tune out, but conversations that are too short can have the same effect on women. If your conversation style is to bark out three pieces of information and then walk away, your message might not be heard either. From one point of view, this is an efficient use of time and you're communicating the most important pieces of information. I get that. From a woman's point of view you have left me wondering, "What the heck?" There's a good chance I'm going to stand there and become preoccupied with thoughts of, "Is he mad at me?" "Was it something I said?" "What's going on?" It can be so distracting that the actual message is completely forgotten, causing a huge communication barrier for you.

As I said earlier, there is no right or wrong way to communicate, but if you want to be an effective communicator it's helpful to take all of these factors into consideration and tailor your conversation strategy accordingly. Give people what they need and they'll give you what you want.

Men: it might not be your personal preference to talk longer than five minutes, but if you simply allow for the possibility that a colleague might need a little extra time and approach the conversation accordingly you'll be better off in the long run. A 10-minute conversation that leads to action and buy-in is better than a five-minute conversation that gets forgotten and becomes a distraction.

Women: less is more in most business conversations. Plan quicker conversations and draft shorter emails. It might feel like you're leaving something out, but that's okay. Men respond to short exchanges and the conversation will continue until they have the necessary information. It might not be your preferred way to communicate, but it keeps them engaged and ensures your message gets heard.

To that end, I would like to offer a solution to bridging the gap between two hours and five minutes. I want you to think of conversations 15-seconds at a time.

No, that is not a typo. 15-seconds. That's all it takes.

I know the look on your face right now. The one that says, "Huh? You're nuts! That's not possible." But let me explain.

Fifteen-seconds might seem like a ridiculous and arbitrary number, but it's actually a number that's quite common in writing for television broadcasts. Prior to starting my on-air career, I spent six years as a sports producer for KING-TV, the local NBC affiliate in Seattle. It was there that I learned the real meaning of "every second counts." On average, I was given two minutes and 30 seconds to cover an entire day of sports news. My job was to give viewers the most important headlines, show them the best highlights and make sure they were up to speed on Seattle-area sports. On a busy night I might have to preview an upcoming Seahawks game, show highlights from the Mariners and Sonics (before they moved to Oklahoma City), and give an injury update about a member of the Washington Huskies football team. All of that had to fit into a two-minute and 30 second time frame.

To get the job done, I couldn't spend too much time on any one story and when I wrote the scripts I could only include the most relevant details. I made every second count by thinking of stories in 15- to 20-second increments. This is very common among TV producers who are taught to write "tight" copy or scripts. The shortest scripts in a broadcast are usually 15-seconds long and often the longer scripts are built on 15-second increments. If you were to look at a show "rundown" – which is like the blueprint or outline for a nightly newscast – you would see scripts that are 15-seconds, 30-seconds, 45-seconds, 60-seconds long and so on. As a general rule in my sportscasts, I did not have a story that ran longer than 90-seconds – that length of time was reserved for special features. With other sports stories to cover I still had to have time for a couple highlights and scores.

Those years as a producer taught me the value of a few seconds and the art of efficient and effective communication. A 15-second script equals about three sentences. And, no, I'm not talking about long run-on sentences, but sentences that look like this:

- "Earl Thomas became the highest paid safety in the NFL today. The Seahawks signed the three-time Pro Bowler to a four-year, $40 million contract extension. Thomas has recorded 15 interceptions since entering the league in 2010."

When read at a comfortable, conversational pace it would take a TV anchor about 15-seconds to read that script.

Viewers won't get every detail about Earl Thomas' new contract, but there's enough information to keep viewers informed. Those who want more details will seek them out from other sources.

Applying this concept to business conversations accomplishes a few things:

1. It bridges the two-hour, five-minute gap

2. It encourages a back-and-forth exchange

3. It avoids the need for too much information

Approaching conversations 15-seconds at a time forces the more talkative folks, like me, to be more judicious with my words and communicate the most important details of my message. For the more introverted crowd, something we haven't addressed up to this point, 15-seconds takes away the pressure of having to engage in long conversations. Short exchanges appeal to the information-seeking group of listeners (usually men). They appreciate this communication style and when they generate a response back it makes the connection-seeking group of listeners (usually women) happy. A back-and-forth exchange built 15-seconds at a time can lead to a very productive minute and a half conversation.

Here's an example of what a conversation would look like using this 15-second approach:

> Co-worker: "I'm so glad we're done with that presentation. I've spent every night the last week working on the PowerPoint slides. I'm ready to move on to something else; how about you?"

You: "You did a great job on the slides, and no offense, but I'm tired of looking at them. I'm hoping to take a break and maybe hit the slopes tomorrow after work. Do you have plans?"

Co-worker: "My kids have a basketball tournament this weekend so we'll be busy with that. I don't ski, but I heard there was a good snow last night. Hope it makes for some good conditions for you."

This entire conversation could last 45-seconds, but take a look at all the different things happening. It's building rapport, and establishing a connection by getting away from "shop talk" or "work talk" and there's built-in follow up opportunities because there are new things to talk about the following Monday and information to file away for future use (i.e. your interest in skiing and the fact that your co-worker's kids play basketball).

But Wait!
At this point, I bet some of you are thinking, "This is never going to work. I have plenty of conversations during the course of the day that last longer than this and they're just fine."

You're right, and there's more to it than that.

These guidelines are meant to be additional tools for you to use in business interactions. Having an idea of where people are coming from helps you become a more effective communicator all the way around. I'm not saying that you should walk around with a stopwatch and time every exchange. I do want you to think about ways you can make it easier for others to listen.

I also want to point out that these guidelines are not meant to take the place of your own common sense or expertise. Here's what I mean by that. If you're the keynote presenter at a conference you are obviously not going to talk in 15-second increments. You might however remember to use both numbers and stories to reach all members of your audience. If you are in a one-on-one meeting with your manager, you might need to give an explanation that is longer than three sentences.

Use common sense.

What I find most often is that when the conversation turns to the business at hand it's easier to relax and rely on your expertise on the subject. Those conversations tend to be a little easier and more familiar. It's the small talk that becomes awkward, or the conversations that lead up to the business talk. That's where these guidelines are particularly helpful. Having a general framework in place to speak someone's language prevents you from walking into a situation totally blind. You might not have a history with the potential client you're meeting with, but you at least have a few general conversation guidelines to work with.

Productivity

Conversations without a measure of productivity could end up being a waste of time. That's why we need a definition and a set of criteria that helps measure productive conversations and that's what we'll cover in the next chapter.

Chapter Recap

Everyone has a different communication style. Use these key takeaways to become a more effective communicator.

Speak in a way others understand

Prepare for different communication styles

Engage in 15-second conversations

Account for both information and connection in conversations

Keep personal preferences in mind

"There is no right or wrong way to communicate, but some approaches are more effective than others."

Chapter 3 –
Small Talk &
Productivity

"Daily small talk does impact your overall productivity at work. It lays the foundation and sets the tone for future interactions."

"Hey Lloyd, what's wrong with Robinson Cano?"

The media had barely been ushered into the manager's office at Safeco Field for our daily session with Mariners manager Lloyd McClendon when one of the newspaper reporters posed that question.

"I don't even get a 'Hi, Lloyd how are you? Good to see you.'" McClendon quipped as a response. "You just come in here and start firing away with your questions and expect me to answer."

There was an amount of playfulness in McClendon's tone, but with or without the humor he helped underscore an important part of an effective conversation strategy – small talk.

Before you skip ahead to the next chapter to get on with something "more important" I want to remind you that the best business relationships are always based on something more than business. Always.

In 2009, Ken Griffey Jr. returned to Seattle to finish his career in the same place it started, with the Mariners. I did not live in Seattle during his first stint with the team and had never met Junior. I was sent to Spring Training for two weeks that February. My job was to collect interviews with a number of players, including Junior. The first day I was in the clubhouse I walked right over to him and introduced myself.

"Hello Ken," I said. "My name is Jen and I work for Fox Sports Northwest. I'll be doing a lot of interviews during the season and I'd like to get an interview with you at some point in the next two weeks."

I smiled as I finished my introduction and he stared at me.

"I'm not talking to you today," was all he said.

"That's alright," I responded. "I'll be here for a couple weeks; we can schedule the interview anytime."

Every day for the next 10 days, I walked up to Junior and said "Hello." Every day his response was the same: "I'm not talking to you today." At that point I would smile politely and stand with the rest of the media members around his locker in the clubhouse. We would listen as he told stories about his off-season vacations, his house in Florida, his golf game and how he was studying to take a pilot's test that would allow him to fly a bigger plane. It was fascinating, but none of it was on tape or part of an interview. As I neared the end of my two-week stay, I started to get nervous. I wondered if I was going to get the interview, and contemplated what would happen if I didn't.

Then one morning I walked into the clubhouse, said "Hello" and was surprised to hear the response, "I'm ready to talk to you today."

From that point forward, Junior was available any time I needed an interview. I never had to wait 10 days to get him to answer a question. In fact, he was so talkative, I had to allow extra time in my schedule if I planned to talk to him. A couple months into the season, I asked why it took so long for him to agree to an interview with me. He looked at me and said, "Because I didn't know you. I didn't know if I could trust you and I didn't know if I liked you."

My relationship with one of the greatest baseball players in the history of the game couldn't be built on questions about his greatness or his career accomplishments and statistics. It came down to listening to him talk about his life outside of baseball and seeing that I had an interest in him as a person.

You have to be willing to talk about something more than work, let people get to know you a little bit, to build trust and rapport. The person who only talks about work will eventually fade into the background and be an annoying hum at the back of the room. You learn to ignore those people – even if they have something to say – because it just gets tiring.

Let's move the example outside of the office for just a second. Consider the friend who only calls when he or she needs something, like a ride to the airport or help watching the kids for a couple hours. They never call just to chat or to ask you to coffee or invite you to lunch. The only call that's made requires you to do something that might not be convenient for you. At first you want to be a good friend so you willingly and even gladly agree. As the pattern repeats itself, however, you find yourself less and less willing to agree and then just avoid having any conversations at all. When the number of that "friend" comes across the caller I.D. you ignore it and go about your day.

In a corporate setting you probably don't have the luxury of ignoring people you don't want to talk to, but there are plenty of times that you can chose the time frame in which you'll respond. For example, I worked with a very talented and dedicated colleague whose single-minded focus on the task at hand was be admired. But it could also be very costly. He was so driven to complete items on his checklist that he was often unaware of how his dedication came across as overwhelming and in some cases neurotic. There were days I arrived at work and not even made it to my desk before he was asking about a story I was working on or if I could help him with something in our show for that day. He was well within his boundaries to ask about both things, but I'd like to at least put my purse down and grab a cup of coffee before I get started. Here's where this can be costly. If I was having a bad day or a particularly stressful day, or I just didn't want to deal with people (it happens to all of us) the last thing I would want to encounter at work is this rapid-fire line of questioning the minute I walk in the door. On those mornings, I might sit in my car a little longer or take the long way around the building to get to my desk, or if there's an email exchange going on, it might take me longer to respond because I just didn't want to deal with it.

The work always gets done in the end, but there are plenty of times it could have been done with less stress and in a more timely manner if my colleague would have recognized that relationships are just as important as skill and the desire to get the job done.

That's true in any office setting and every locker room I've ever been in. Athletes have to be comfortable and willing to talk to me win or lose. I've experienced few things that are more intimidating than walking into an NFL locker room after a tough loss. It's far from glamorous when you're face-to-face with 53 sweaty, physically imposing, exhausted and pissed off men who would rather do anything than talk about the game they just played. They see me coming and they know my only job is to ask them to analyze the game using language suitable for a radio audience.

A bad game or a tough loss is an athlete's version of a bad day at the office. If the only time I approach a player is following a game to talk about what happened on the field they look at me the same way you'd look at that friend who just asked you for the umpteenth favor in a row. The conversations I have with the players during the week about their families, college teams and hobbies are just as important as the ones I have during live post-game interviews.

And if you don't believe me, let's consider a survey published by the American Psychological Association (APA) in 2012.[2] The survey found that employees who feel valued are more likely to work harder and be more engaged at work. That's not necessarily a surprise, but the numbers associated with the survey are staggering. Of the respondents who said they feel valued at work, 93 percent of them said they are motivated to do their best work and 88 percent reported feeling engaged. Compare that to the group of respondents who do not feel valued at work. Only 33 percent of those employees are motivated to do their best work and just 38 percent said they felt engaged at work. There is a significant drop off between 93 percent and 33 percent. It is no doubt costing employers a lot of money and leading to increased stress for employees trying to pick up the slack.

The survey respondents were asked what would increase their feeling of value at work and you can probably guess their responses: increased pay, more flexible work hours and more influence in decision making at work.

I'm sure all of those things could lead to happier employees who feel more valued and work harder, but sometimes it's not possible to deliver. There is,

---

[2] https://www.apa.org/news/press/releases/2012/03/well-being.aspx

however, something that you and I can do every day to add value to the people around us: listen.

The same year that survey was released, the Seattle Seahawks played the Green Bay Packers in a Monday Night Football game in Seattle. It is important to note here that the regular officials were on strike and fans had mounting anguish towards the referees going into this game. The Seahawks trailed 12–7 with eight seconds remaining in the game. A national audience watched anxiously as Seahawks quarterback Russell Wilson launched a final pass attempt into the end zone. I was on the sidelines for the radio broadcast and it felt like everyone in the stadium held their breath waiting to see what would happen. After what seemed like an eternity Seahawks receiver Golden Tate came down with the ball landing amid chaos and controversy. It was ruled a "simultaneous catch" between Tate and Packers' safety M.D. Jennings. The end result was a touchdown for the Seahawks, but many football fans across the country disagreed with the ruling. The Seahawks won the game 14–12 and fans outside of Seattle started calling it the "Fail Mary" game. (A "Hail Mary" in football refers to a final pass attempt, usually made in desperation, to try and win at the end of the game.)

On the field, without TV commentary and multiple replays, I didn't realize the extent of the outrage or controversy until I got into the locker room and heard the questions coming from the national media. I was even more surprised to learn that in the days following that game, more than 70,000 fans called the NFL League office. Why? Were they hoping to get the call reversed? Was the league going to change the outcome of the game because fans called and complained? No, but the fans wanted their voices heard.

And the same thing played out at Seahawks headquarters in Renton, Washington. I walked in for practice later that week and was greeted by the receptionist with a wave of her hand instead of a usual "Hi Jen, how's it going?" Her ear was pressed to the phone and she whispered, "The fans won't stop calling and I can't get a word in. I try to transfer them to the appropriate person, but they won't stop talking to me."

Why did that happen? Because the fans wanted someone to listen.

I promise football fans aren't the only ones who want someone to listen to them. Your co-workers, colleagues, clients, family and friends all want someone to listen to them as well. If you are the person who fills that role, you instantly add value and can start reaping the benefits.

Daily small talk does impact your overall productivity at work. Imagine what would happen if everyone around you was giving their best effort. How much easier would your job become? How much more pleasant would it be in your office? How much time could you save in having a job done right the first time instead of having to troubleshoot and redo it?

Small talk at work is a way to lay the foundation and set the tone for future interactions. It's similar to the way a football coach views plays in the first quarter of a game. The first few plays of a game aren't talked about nearly as much as the momentum shifting plays in the second half, the game–winning drive in the fourth quarter or the huge penalty that cost a team its chance at a win.

If you talk to any NFL coach however, they'll say the first 15 plays of a game are critical when it comes to setting the tone and establishing a successful game plan. Everything that happens in a game is predicated on those first few plays. They're so important that most coaches script out the first 15 plays. They do this after watching film of their own team, film of the opponents and then identifying their best chances for success. Scripting the first 15 plays gives them a chance to rely on their game plan without making knee–jerk decisions to start a game. It allows them to get a feel for how the game is going to play out and provides a sample size that can be used to make adjustments.

Developing a strategy for productive small talk is the equivalent of a coach scripting out the first 15 plays. It allows you to (1) get a feel for the situation, (2) set the tone for the exchange, (3) put yourself in a position to succeed later in the conversation and (4) gives you a way to measure success.

In order to do that, however, we need a way to define productivity.

Measuring Productive Conversations

We covered "Topic" and "Timing" in Chapter 2, but without guidelines on what makes a conversation productive you could still be missing out on effective conversation strategies.

As a "Type A" personality I like to follow a process, know that I'm doing something right and not wasting time. That's why I came up with this definition of a productive conversation.

A productive conversation is one that:

1. Establishes a connection

2. Builds rapport

3. Creates follow up opportunities

Conversations that don't include these elements could not only be a waste of time, but lead to lost revenue and missed opportunities. I frequently give presentations for professionals in the banking and financial services industry. I asked a friend who worked with high net-worth individuals how long it took to gain a new client from the time of introduction until he or she was signing papers to work with his firm. He told me that on average it took 18 months.

We talked through all the different ways he would reach out to potential clients, and the kind of interactions he would have throughout those 18 months. My friend is very talented and skilled at closing deals so his conversion rate of potential clients to actual clients is very high. But there is a risk with this type of work. If the ongoing communication isn't hitting the mark, it's possible to get several months into this process and believe that everything is going smoothly, only to find out the potential client is going elsewhere. If that happens it leads to not only a loss of money, but a loss of time as well.

It takes time for all business relationships to develop and knowing how to hit the mark on productive conversations from the outset means you're not wasting time during that process. Understanding the components of a productive conversation is especially important in networking situations. But any conversation gives you an opportunity to be productive and feel more comfortable.

That's usually the first sign you've made a connection. There's a clear spark and appreciation for a common interest. It doesn't need to be a deep connection. It's just a starting point to build rapport, which is the second element of a productive conversation. By the way, the definition of rapport is: a close and harmonious relationship in which the people or groups concerned understand each other's feelings or ideas and communicate well.

That definition seems a little intense in the context of networking or considering different scenarios that require small talk. If it were up to me, I'd add the comment "you know it when you feel it." Here's what rapport feels like in my line of work. I know that I have a rapport with a player when I can approach him and ask for an interview, win or lose, and know he'll graciously do the interview. Rapport is also the feeling you get when you feel comfortable making an introduction to someone.

There are lots of other ways to describe and think about rapport, but realize this: you can have a connection without rapport. There are more than 70 wine tasting rooms about 10 minutes from my house in the Seattle area. My husband and I have spent many weekends sipping wine and on occasion we strike up conversations with the couples around us. We could spend a couple hours chatting over wine because there's a connection, but we have never become friends with any of those couples. Our conversation was just a nice way to pass the time on a lazy weekend afternoon. There was no rapport and there was no need to follow up.

That person that you sit next to on the plane who engages in chitchat just to be polite might make a connection, but if the conversation was awkward, uncomfortable or unnecessary you'll likely part ways at the arrival gate and be on your way.

There are two points I'm getting at here. First, it takes more than a connection to make a conversation count. The fact that you are in the same place at the same time as another person is a connection point, but if you can't follow up that observation with something worth talking about, there won't be an additional exchange.

Second, there are times when it's okay that you won't connect with them further. The cashier at the grocery store doesn't expect you to build rapport. You don't need to talk to every stranger you see in an elevator. Simply being polite to the barista who serves you coffee is just fine. The goal here is to be equipped with the tools needed to have a productive conversation at any given moment, because you don't always know where your next big opportunity is coming from. It's up to you to use common sense and test your skills in the appropriate settings.

We know that connection and rapport are key in productive conversations, but the most important element is the third part of that definition – "creates follow up opportunities." It's the part that most people forget, or never even consider, but it's the secret sauce in building relationships. That's really the goal of productive conversations and useful small talk. It takes multiple exchanges and interactions to build relationships and you need a conversation topic that lends itself to follow up opportunities. If you're already running down a list of your most popular go-to small talk topics, let me just say that the weather shouldn't be on it. What kind of follow up does that have?

Before we work through that topic together, I'll pose the same question to you that I ask my live audiences. What are the four topics that are off the table when you're chatting with someone you don't know well or you know only in a work setting? These are the subjects that tend to be hot-button topics. Keep in mind we're trying to build relationships here, not make people angry.

Did these four topics come to mind? Money, religion, politics and sex. If you work in banking or finance you might object to money being on the list, but remember we're talking in terms of small talk and conversation starters. Money is your industry and your job. When the conversation turns to business you can talk about dollars and cents all you need to, but if you're meeting someone for the first time you're not going to ask about their personal finances or the tax bracket they filed under this year.

Let's keep going on our list of taboo small talk topics. If you try to talk about headlines on the front page of the newspaper or things you might see on The Daily Show, what will you end up talking about? Probably money, religion, politics and sex. So current events and front-page news are likely off the table as small talk topics.

How about the go-to conversation starter for most people who have no idea where to start? The weather. I live in Seattle. Do you know what the weather is like here? Nine months out of the year it is cold, grey, wet and dreary. Not exactly what I'd like to talk about, and who cares what the weather is doing anyway? I certainly don't want to use it as a follow up opportunity because it doesn't change as much as the meteorologists would like you to think and I don't care about the weather. I care about the person I'm talking to and I need a piece of information that gives me some insight and causes me to make a mental note as to when and how I'm going to talk with them again. Let me put it this way – I talk to cab drivers about the weather, not potential business contacts.

Keep this in mind when you're trying to find your follow up opportunities in a conversation. On average, I've found it takes five different exchanges with an athlete to get to the point where we can have an honest and comfortable interview. I have found that average to be about right when it comes to establishing new business connections or getting to the point where I can work comfortably with a co-worker. So your conversation topic should have some legs and be able to get you through five separate exchanges on your way to building a relationship.

As a point of clarification, I'm not saying that you shouldn't know about current events or the most recent stock market trends or that you shouldn't be aware of the big snowstorm moving into the area in the next 24 hours. All of that knowledge is useful and necessary. Any of those subjects could be used to start a conversation, but you might not like where those conversations go.

If you're trying to make a good first impression at a networking event, or trying to remind a potential client how pleasant you are to be around, do you really want to run the risk of starting a heated debate around politics, morals, ethics or foreign policy? You might enjoy those types of exchanges with someone you already know, but it's probably not something you'd like to dive into with someone you're trying to connect with.

The weather isn't a hot button topic – unless you end up discussing global warming – but talking about the weather can easily turn into a relatively short, unproductive conversation that becomes a dead end.

And that's the way many people start. With a dead end. Then when the conversation comes to an awkward end they think, "What's the point of small talk? That was a waste of my time." Because the weather is a topic we've been trained to use to make "adequate" small talk, that awkward feeling and uncomfortable situation repeats itself over and over, slowly reinforcing the idea that small talk is useless.

Only it's not.

It's a vital part of business and workplace communication, and it should start with sports.

Chapter Recap

Daily conversations can go a long way in helping co-workers feel valued. Increase your productivity by adding value and remembering these key takeaways.

Validate co-workers by listening

Allow time for small talk

Leave the weather out of the conversation

Understand people who feel valued work harder

Evaluate conversations based on productive definition

"It takes time for all business relationships to develop and knowing how to hit the mark on productive conversations from the outset means you're not wasting time during that process."

Chapter 4 –
Why Sports?

"Sports works. It's more versatile. It appeals to more people. It's more multifaceted than any other topic, and it leads to more opportunities. It's up to you to make the most of them."

"Why did you stop four feet behind the car in front of us?" I asked my husband.

"As a conversation starter," he replied.

"What? That's dumb."

"Is it? You're talking to me right now."

I had to give him credit. It wasn't the best conversation starter in the world, but we were talking and it did make me laugh. It also highlights this point: if your goal is just to get a response, just about any conversation starter will work. If your goal is to build relationships and create business opportunities, you need to be more strategic in your thinking.

In the previous chapter we looked at the importance of small talk when it comes to adding value to the people around you and increasing productivity, (theirs and yours). We also ran through six topics (money, religion, politics, sex, front page headlines and weather) that aren't recommended when striking up a conversation that you hope leads to a business relationship.

So where does that leave us? With sports, of course.

You had to know that was coming. I am a sports broadcaster, after all, and the title of the book gives you a pretty good hint. But my advocacy of using sports as the go-to conversation starter in business goes way beyond my sports fandom or profession. Sports works like no other conversation topic because of its ability to connect you to a large network of people and because of the viewing habits of the fans. Don't believe me? Consider this:

It Meets Our Conversation Criteria. Sports conversations can easily fit into a 15-second conversation window and include information that appeals to anyone you're talking to. Statistics for the information minded? Check. How about the fans that want to talk about the big picture outcome of a game, or the atmosphere at the stadium and are primarily looking for a way to connect with others instead of sharing statistics? You can easily talk about sports in those terms as well.

In addition, sports are generally considered a "safe" subject. There are enough different aspects of a game or season to stay away from controversy and find follow up opportunities that help us ensure productive conversations.

It's DVR-Proof. There was a time, not too long ago, that television shows dominated the water-cooler conversations at work. Think back to the late 90's and NBC's Thursday night television lineup dubbed "Must See TV." Shows like Friends, Seinfeld and ER not only dominated the overnight ratings, but conversations on Friday. If you didn't watch on Thursday night, you were left out. But the television landscape changed dramatically in the 2000's. VCRs were replaced by recording devices like DVRs; viewers were introduced to on-demand programing and viewing sites like Hulu and Netflix. In addition, the number of cable channels available increased and fragmented viewing audiences even more.

As a result, it's harder to capture real-time viewing audiences. At my house, for example, episodes of my favorite weekly shows like NCIS could sit on my DVR for weeks until I have a chance to watch them. This not only causes problems for advertisers, but also eliminates popular TV shows as a potential daily conversation topic.

Here's the advantage sports provides – it will never be viewed that way. No fan would wait three weeks to find out the outcome of a game. A fan might record a game to watch later in the day or to re-watch at a later time, but he or she would have seen highlights or at the very least the score within a short period of time after the game. Remember that sporting events happen every day, and knowing that fans track outcomes every day gives you fresh conversation topics. If you follow sports headlines, you won't be left standing in awkward silence wondering what to say.

Provides Follow up Opportunities. Sports seasons last for months at a time. Each sport plays a number of regular season games ranging from 16 in the National

Football League to 162 in Major League Baseball. That doesn't even count off-season activities like training camps and drafts or post-season playoff games. The sheer number of games and events can seem tiring and overwhelming at times, especially with increased media coverage of most of them. But try thinking about each game as a chance to engage with a fan you're trying to connect with or work with. Now those long seasons are opportunities to strengthen relationships and build business.

The ongoing nature of sports provides not only follow up opportunities, but also a warm lead every time you reach out to a fan.

Customizable. Sports provides a number of different avenues to follow during a conversation. Think about the Super Bowl game for a minute. How many different things do you hear fans talking about around the time of the "big game?" You could talk about the commercials, the parties, the food at the parties, the half time performers, the prop bets, the location of the game, the teams actually playing in the game, the cities those teams are located in and the results of the game. There's something there for everyone.

The Super Bowl is one of the biggest and best examples of how sports conversations go beyond what happens on the field, but nearly every game or event offers similar conversation topics. You might not throw a party for a regular season baseball game, but you can still talk about the food at the ballpark or the celebrity who threw out the first pitch.

Being able to customize your conversations does more than just allow you to talk about a part of the game that interests you. It also lets you cater to what fans want to talk about and gives you more opportunities to learn about the people around you.

Grants Access. Sports fans talk to other sports fans. It's as simple as that. From executives to recent college grads and the cleaning staff to the chief of staff – sports fans are part of a community and they're happy to share their enthusiasm, frustration, opinions and fandom with others in that community.

That means it doesn't matter whom you're trying to connect with or get an introduction to; if he or she is a sports fan you have common ground and access to talk to that person.

Offers Personal Branding Opportunities. The way you talk about a game says a lot about you. Are you a gracious winner or a sore loser? Do you have a tendency to blame a loss on a bad call, or do you give the coach the benefit of the doubt on a controversial decision? It's easy to think that doesn't matter and it's all part of the game, but in general these reactions are based on innate personality traits. Often the way fans react to a game or an outcome is the same way they respond to similar situations at work.

The benefit of knowing this is that you can actually give more insight about yourself in a sports conversation than you realize. People around you will pick up on your comments – good or bad – and use that to form opinions about you. Make the most of conversation opportunities by talking in a way that reflects your values and positive characteristics.

You see this frequently in post–game interviews with athletes and coaches. I can tell you after spending a lot of time around Pete Carroll and the Seahawks, their messaging after a game is purposefully delivered. If there's a questionable call by the officials there's a specific way they will talk about it during post–game interviews so that everyone is on the same page and saying the same thing.

It's the same concept when you're trying to express your personal values. When talking about a specific game, favorite team or player, decide what message you want to get across about yourself. For example, if you want to highlight your resiliency in being able to bounce back after a rough sales quarter, you make a tie to Peyton Manning and his ability to bounce back from neck surgery in 2011 and set the record for most career touchdown passes thrown in the history of the NFL just three years later. Your statement could be something like this: "I'm really impressed with the resiliency Peyton Manning has shown in bouncing back from his neck surgery a couple years ago. I had a bounce back of my own after a tough first quarter this year."

I think those factors make a pretty compelling case for why sports works in conversations. That's not to say it's the only thing you can ever talk about, but it is a more foolproof subject than people realize.

When I'm giving a presentation, it's not uncommon for someone to raise their hand and say something like this, "I can see sports working, but if I'm trying to network with someone I usually just ask questions about them. Everyone likes to talk about themselves." As the comment is being made, I look around the room and see heads nodding in agreement. A few seconds later someone else will chime in and say, "Or family. I ask about their kids and what's going on at home."

Both are very popular approaches and both can work, but they can also backfire. Remember we're focusing on conversations with people you don't know very well.

In those situations, I've seen the Goldilocks paradigm play out more times than I can count. You either get too much information or too little and rarely find that "just right" combination that includes a rapport–building connection and an opportunity to talk business.

"But wait," you're thinking. "I thought I was supposed to be taking an interest in the people around me, adding value and all that. What if they want to talk about their family or their weekend hobbies?"

Good question. If that's what they want to talk about, then by all means give them an opportunity to do so. But I would also recommend giving them a chance to warm up to you. If the first thing you do upon meeting someone is hit them with a question like, "What's going on with your family these days?" or "Nice to meet you, do you have any kids?" you're not likely to get the same response as if you ease your way into the personal element.

For example if I pose the question, "Did you see the finish in the Seahawks game Sunday?" to a new business connection, it allows him to say, "Only the highlights. My son had an all-day soccer tournament and we didn't get home until late. But I loved seeing that win."

When I'm trying to build relationships I want as many different opportunities to connect as I can find. That quick exchange opens the door for conversations about the son who plays soccer, his soccer season, the Seahawks, football in general and if I wanted to broaden out even more, I could ask if he has other children. Not only can I pick and choose what I want to talk about next, but I have multiple topics to use in future follow up conversations.

Contrary to popular belief, not everyone wants to talk about themselves or their families. Some of the most successful, interesting, well-spoken people I have ever met will become suddenly silent when asked direct questions about their personal lives.

In fact, most of the athletes I cover would prefer not to talk about their skills or their accomplishments. They find it much easier to talk about their teammates or the team in general. If I ask about their impressive contribution to a game like a mammoth home run, they're more likely to downplay it and shift their comments and their focus to the solid performance by their starting pitcher.

I run into a similar dynamic when interacting with high-level executives. While some of them are very comfortable in the spotlight and enjoy highlighting their success, many I've met would prefer to downplay their role. When I recognize that situation, I know that asking them questions about their life, their success or their hobbies isn't a good way to get them to open up. Those all feel like very personal questions and if I'm not already a trusted colleague or friend, they don't see a reason to divulge such information.

I'm not the only one who deals with those situations. I've met executives who understand how to cater the conversation to get results too. About a year ago, I received a call out of the blue on a Friday afternoon prior to a big weekend of college football and NFL games. "Hello Jen, you don't know me, but my name is Tom and I want to tell you I think you're brilliant."

After an opening sentence like that, how could I resist listening to what he had to say? (Note to readers: I've found this is a very effective way to start a conversation with me.)

He continued by saying, "I've been to your website and I couldn't agree more with your concept of using sports as the go-to conversation topic. I have used sports a number of times to interact with executives and I just got off the phone with a CEO who typically doesn't talk very much. I used sports and he stayed on the phone for 15 minutes."

The gentleman who called me was Tom Kardashian, the former President of Great Western Meat Packing Company, co-founder of the Hollywood newspaper, Radio and Records, and current business and professional coach in the Los Angeles area. The CEO he had just talked to was my father, Steve Mueller, at Southwestern Energy.

When Tom revealed he had been talking to my father, I understood his challenge immediately. My father is brilliant. He's a strong leader and a hard worker. He's traveled the world and has interesting hobbies, but he's not much of a talker. Don't get me wrong. He's skilled at giving presentations, a gracious host at a party and an enjoyable dinner guest quick with a joke or a dry witted comment. But given his druthers, and all else being equal, my father does not talk for fun.

His tolerance for small talk is at the low end of the spectrum, and asking open ended questions like, "How's it going?" or "How is your family?" will likely lead to polite but short responses. My father falls in the category of someone seeking information in conversation. Keeping him on the phone for 15 minutes was a significant accomplishment by Tom. As he and I chatted, Tom explained that he used the upcoming football game as a starting point to the conversation and then included questions about me, who he knew from previous conversations with my father, worked on the Seahawks broadcast, and my brother who he also knew was a big sports fan.

The reason for Tom's phone call that day was just to stay in touch. My father, upon hearing the story, dryly commented that Tom called to win a bet that he could keep the conversation going for 15 minutes. There is mutual respect between my father and Tom and they have several common business connections, but they currently don't do business together.

Executing a Strategy

There are a few things I want to highlight about Tom's approach in talking with my father and how he used the "sports talk playbook" to his advantage:

1) **He used timely sporting events to initiate the call.** Southwestern Energy is headquartered in Houston, Texas. It's a football–crazy state, and not a stretch to think my father knew which games were coming up.

2) **He used sports to bridge a communication gap.** Tom is a talker. My father would prefer to keep conversations short and information driven. Asking a specific question about the game made it possible to engage my father and fulfill Tom's desire to connect.

3) **He used sports to transition into other subjects.** A conversation that started about football gave Tom a chance to ask about the Seahawks game that week, my job with the team and then the rest of the family.

4) **He created additional conversation opportunities.** A few months after that call, the Seahawks won the Super Bowl. I know that at least one interaction between Tom and my father included talk of that game.

5) **He used football as a way to stay on the radar.** They currently don't do business together, but that doesn't mean that will always be the case. Staying top of mind is helpful if and when an opportunity arises in the future.

I also find it fascinating that both Tom and my father are both executives at a comparable level. Meaning Tom is not a mid–level manager or even a senior manager trying to interact with the CEO of a company. Speaking in a way that people want to hear and will respond to is important regardless of who you are, your position within a company and your overall status. Tom has enough business clout of his own that it would be reasonable to assume people would just listen to what he has to say regardless of his communication style. But Tom is smart enough to know that status is only part of the equation; it might get someone to take your call, but getting them to stay on the phone for 15 minutes requires a strategy.

Every conversation you have is influenced by differences in communication styles and personality types in general. Having sports at your disposal to use in conversation gives you a versatile tool to more easily overcome those differences.

Remember the example from the beginning of the chapter? Just about anything can be used to start a conversation, but not all topics are equal.

Sports works. It's more versatile. It appeals to more people. It's more multifaceted than any other topic, and it leads to more opportunities. It's up to you to make the most of them.

Chapter Recap

Sports is one of the most versatile conversation topics you can find. Here are key takeaways on why sports works in small talk conversations:

Wide ranging options for personal branding and follow up opportunities

Has daily drama/story lines

You get access to every sports fan regardless of title or position

Chapter 5 –
Leveraging Sports Fandom

"Leveraging fandom is more than using sports metaphors or general sports concepts. It's tapping into a specific fan base and using their passion to drive conversations and responses."

"It's such a waste of time to watch games."

"I prefer to talk about more important things."

"I think athletes are greedy and make too much money."

"If you ask me, talking sports alienates women."

I've heard all of these reasons and many more from people making a case as to why they don't follow sports. I've even encountered companies that have issued a ban on talking sports at work for some of those reasons. One corporation in particular told me that sports metaphors were prohibited during the business day because it "perpetuated the perception that the financial industry was predominately made up of white males. In addition, sports alienated a large number of employees, particularly the women."

I understand that not everyone is a fan, but you don't have to be a fan to utilize the passion of others. This is not a male vs. female issue. This is a matter of business. Do you want to have all the tools at your disposal to make a sale? Secure a new client? Advance your career? Build better relationships? Show your value?

If you answered "yes" to any of those questions then you should understand how to use sports to your advantage. In addition, trying to ban sports talk or sports metaphors at work is a waste of time.

For many fans, sports are so ingrained in who they are it's unlikely a company policy would prevent them from talking about a game or making a sports reference. In addition, would you rather have co-workers and employees focusing on their jobs or concentrating on how to not make a sports reference during the day? (Trust me, as a lifelong Houston Astros fan and a sports broadcaster who has covered many losing teams and struggling franchises, if a few losing seasons can't dissuade a fan from coming to a game or professing a love for the team, a company mandate certainly won't do the trick.)

It's far more effective to offer suggestions on how to use sports as an advantage in business. Sports sells. We see that all the time in athletes advertising products from cars to headphones to teams selling sponsorships and fans buying merchandise.

And we should be seeing it more in every industry, every corporation and every workplace setting. After all, we are seeing a steady increase of fans throughout the sports landscape, and in the NFL in particular.

- Gallup poll trends since 2000 indicate between 56 and 63 percent of Americans describe themselves as "sports fans." The surveys included men and women from the ages of 18 to 50 and over. (So, if you tend to think that sports are a topic just for men, you're not looking at the numbers or the big picture.)

- According to a 2014 Associated Press–Gfk poll, 49 percent of Americans say they're NFL fans.

- According to Neilson TV ratings, 111.5 million people watched the Seattle Seahawks beat the Denver Broncos in Super Bowl XLVIII, making it the most watched TV program in U.S. history.

- According to Scarborough Research in 2013, women represent approximately 45 percent of the NFL fan base.

These are just a few of the numbers in the sea of data collected on sports fans, but it's enough to show three key points:

1. Non–sports fans are becoming the minority.

2. Sports are not a male–only interest.

3. There are millions of sports fans with a passion that can be put to work for you.

Sports fans aren't just fans on game days. They're fans every day of the week. They want to talk about their team or their favorite player or the big headline making news across the country. Leveraging fandom in business means you're making it useful in creating business opportunities, strengthening your position or advancing your career. It's using existing sports passion for the purpose of building rapport and getting results.

Leveraging fandom is more than using sports metaphors or general sports concepts. It's tapping into a specific fan base and using their passion to drive conversations and responses. Trying to temper the passion of a fan won't lead to results, but knowing how to exploit that passion will.

The first step in leveraging sports fandom is learning how to limit generic metaphors and customize your approach. The second step is strategizing a business development plan around sports fandom.

The first step can be expressed in this equation:

Specific Sports Element + Transferable Concept x Fans = Rapport + Response

The equation shows that if you start with a specific sports element, add a transferable concept[3], and multiply it by any number of fans, you'll end up with rapport and response.

It's important to understand the elements at play here, because it's more than using cliché phrases like, "that was a home run" or "I guess we're just going to have to try a Hail Mary." Clichés and sports metaphors aren't very effective in leveraging the passion of fans

---

[3] A transferable concept refers to an idea that is found both in sports and business like time management and work ethic.

because they're often overused or misused and lack a personal connection.

We learned in Chapter 3 that personal connections help people feel valued, and people who feel valued at work are more productive. That applies here too. Making a personal connection requires a customized message not an overused cliché.

Think about the landscape of sports today. It's all about customization and specialization from the highly trained athletes themselves to the fans who watch them. Each fan base has a different personality, and different ways to express their fandom. Seattle Seahawks fans are completely different from Green Bay Packers fans or the fans in Jacksonville Florida in the way they cheer, watch games, dress, tailgate and how they manage expectations for the season.

Customize your sports message at work and it will resonate better and be more effective. There are millions of sports fans in the world but they don't want to be treated the same. That's why the equation starts with a "specific sports element." It could be a team, player, headline or game. An example in Jacksonville would be the Jaguars turning to rookie quarterback Blake Bortles last year. An NFL fan in Dallas would prefer to talk about the improvement of the Cowboys' offensive line or the play of their quarterback Tony Romo.

The specific sports element isn't limited to football; anything from the world of sports works, like Rory McIlroy on the PGA Tour, Serena Williams in tennis and the impact of Kevin Durant on the Oklahoma City Thunder.

It's not enough to just find a specific sports element to talk about. Without identifying a transferable concept you become a fan just talking to hear yourself talk. That's one of the reasons I hear from executives who show resistance or pushback to my messaging about sports conversations at work. When I hear things like, "we've taken this sports culture too far" or "we need to start talking about other things around here instead of just sports" I know it's not a sports issue, but a communication issue.

It doesn't matter what subject you talk about if you don't know how to have a productive conversation and communicate effectively. From a leadership perspective if you've got a lot of people talking just to hear themselves talk and there's no actual communication or action being taken, I can understand the resistance to talk sports at work. A transferable concept will allow you to draw a direct connection between your specific sports element and your business, prompting a natural segue into the real meat and potatoes of getting things done.

If you're starting to think about all the ways you can use the "team" or "teamwork" concept, stop right there. That's not it. General comparisons work about as well as overused clichés. You've got to be more creative and specific.

To spark those conversations in Seattle I write weekly blog posts during the football season called "Profit This Season." Every week I take a specific quote from a press conference, describe something I saw in the locker room or highlight a certain aspect of game planning. Then I explain the business application and show Seahawks fans how they could talk about their team even more.

Here's an example: communication is important to any sports team and it's important to any workplace environment. Don't just broad brush that concept and expect it to be useful. Find a specific example of communication and use that as the starting point. Seahawks coach Pete Carroll assigned practice themes for each day of the week. Monday is "Tell the Truth Monday" and it's the day players come in, watch film from Sunday and evaluate what happened. They are forced to tell the truth because the film never lies. It's a form of accountability and it prompts honest discussions over what went well and what needs improvement before the next game.

The sports specific element is Pete Carroll and the Seahawks. The transferable concept is accountability. The next step of our equation is to take the message to the fans.

This is what it might look like. Let's say there's a coffee shop in Seattle that has had a problem with employee performance, finger pointing and lack of results. Instead of ordering change, the owner wants employees to take an honest look at how they're helping or hurting the situation. Several employees are known Seahawks fans.

Instead of starting a staff meeting or dialogue with, "We really need to talk about employee performance···" The owner could say, "What a game yesterday for the Seahawks. I can't believe they didn't pull it out in the fourth quarter. I wonder what showed today up on 'Tell the Truth Monday.' What do you think they talked about during film study today?" After a brief discussion of what happened in the game, it's time to introduce the accountability piece and segue the conversation. "I think it's great that the Hawks have to go in and be honest and accountable for what happened. What if we had a 'Tell the Truth Monday?' What kinds of things do we need to be more accountable for?" That effectively turns the conversation toward the workplace issue at hand.

Making a specific tie-in to the Seahawks creates additional buy-in from the Seahawks fans in the room. It's a customized message just for them. It gives them a legitimate reason to talk about their team when they're at work, show their pride and utilize their fandom. Their excitement for their team helps validate the message and makes them more likely to act on it. That's how you build rapport and generate a response.

Here's another example from the NFL that makes a direct connection between a sports specific element and a transferable concept that applies to business.

The NFL Draft makes sports headlines every spring. There are weeks of build up, combines, tryouts, mock drafts, evaluations and commentary. At first glance it might not seem applicable to your office. Who does mock drafts based on your next potential hires? But look a little closer and you'll see that the draft is nothing more than an employer (in this case a professional football team) looking to find the employee (which happens to be a player) with the right skill set to do the job they need to fill. That's what the NFL Draft, and every other sports league draft, is. It's a team placing value on specific skill sets and determining how much they want to pay for that skill.

The next time you get tired of hearing conversations about an upcoming draft, use the transferable concept of talent evaluation to start a discussion in your office or among your staff.

The following list offers ideas on some of the transferable topics that exist in sports and business. Every sport contains each of these elements. This is not a comprehensive list, but one designed to get you thinking about parallels in your conversations and looking for specific examples:

- Teamwork

- Communication

- Goal setting

- Clutch performances

- Performance review

- Talent evaluation

- Wins vs. losses

- Discipline

- Work ethic

- Preparation

- Unselfishness

- Time management

- Decision making

- Hiring

- Firing

- Executive influence

- Leadership

- Workplace behavior

- Long-term planning

- Salary/contract negotiations

There are many more conversations you could initiate as a result of this list. Every conversation at work doesn't have to start with sports, but it's a good tool to leverage. In my work as a TV and radio sideline reporter I experience the passion of fans every day. I'm on the sidelines and in the middle of all the action for every Seahawks game. The crowd is so loud it's deafening and the passion of the 12s (the nickname for Seahawks fans) is undeniable. I know how those fans impact a game and I wonder how they could impact your efforts.

I also wonder what they're trying to tell you.

Reading Between the Lines
The football conversation that happens before or after a game might seem like a waste of time at work, but the fans engaging in that conversation could be trying to tell you something. Every conversation about a team, player or game offers a glimpse of a fan's personality and communication style. When you know what you're listening for you're in a better position to understand how to work more closely with them and generate more success.

This can be done without scheduling meetings and doing extensive personality tests; all you have to do is be willing to let them talk about a game or express their fandom. Here are five things you can learn as a result:

1. **Are they a team player?** Fans who loyally wear team gear and actively participate in team-related events like training camp, tailgating and player appearances enjoy being part of a community – part of "the team." They likely thrive in group settings and like the camaraderie and connection that comes from being part of a team. This could mean they are good at collaboration and that they will do better working with others, rather than on their own.

2. **What characteristics or values do they prize?** Ask an employee about his or her favorite player and pay attention to the description. The on-field ability and stats are only part of the attraction. For example, you might hear about the poise and leadership of New England quarterback Tom Brady, or the hard-nosed "Beast Mode" running style of Seattle Seahawks running back Marshawn Lynch. If they find those qualities attractive in the football players, they will find them attractive in people they work with and will seek to emulate them also.

3. **How do they respond to a win or a loss?** Listening to the way a fan talks about the outcome of the game can tell you a lot about his/her ability to handle success and failure. Are they gracious winners or sore losers? Do they blame officials? True colors come through when talking about a game. Their reaction to wins and losses at work will be similar to how they express their fandom.

4. **Are they Monday morning quarterbacks?** Second-guessing and criticizing a coaching decision a day or two after the game seems like just part of being a fan, but it is another aspect that is tied to personality traits. An employee who consistently second guesses a coach is more likely to challenge or question authority, which – depending on your organization and the depth of which the person does this – can be a good or a bad trait.

5. **What is their preferred communication style?** We already know that people have different styles and that can be seen in the way each person describes a game. Some people focus on numbers and prefer shorter conversations, while others include more details and favor longer exchanges. How does that work within your organization? Do you acknowledge and accommodate different communication styles?

At this point, it should all be starting to come together: the value of sports, the importance of strategic conversations and how to combine those elements to become a more effective communicator.

Now it's time to explore specific ways to use sports conversations to create business opportunities.

Chapter Recap

Sports fans are fans every day of the week, which gives you an advantage if you can effectively talk sports and remember these key takeaways:

Forget about limiting sports talk at work

Allow colleagues to talk about their passions

Necessary business conversations become easier with transferable sports concepts

Sports appeals to more than half of all Americans

Chapter 6 – Business Building Strategies

"Surveys show more than half of all Americans are sports fans or roughly 159 million people. Use sports to connect to millions of people in business."

"So are you in town for this football stuff?"

I put down my cell phone and turned toward the man who had just claimed the seat next to me at the bar. I was in Indianapolis for the NFL combine and loving the vibe of the city.

"Yes, I am. But I take it that you're not?" I countered.

"No, I'm not a sports fan," the man responded. "I don't get into it. I probably should. I just took a job in sales."

It was the perfect opening for me. I was fascinated by his response and disinterest in sports. I saw it as my chance to evangelize about the importance of sports conversations in business and sales.

We had a pleasant conversation and then he said something that stopped me mid-sentence.

"You know, I do like to cycle." He said slowly, as if it was just dawning on him that cycling was a sport. "I used to enjoy watching Lance Armstrong and I go on a 100-mile and 150-mile ride every year." My mouth dropped open as he went on to explain that he'd competed in triathlons and marathons.

It was right there the whole time: he was a sports fan. He just didn't follow one of the "big four" sports of football, basketball, baseball and hockey. When I pointed this out, he laughed and said he hadn't thought of it that way.

I see this situation play out on a regular basis. Sports are all encompassing. There are certain sports, teams or seasons that get more publicity, but when it comes right down to it everyone is a fan of something. It might be dog shows, the Olympics, a child's little league team, or any number of other organized activities, but it's rare for a person to have no connection to sports.

We saw a little of that in the last chapter when I mentioned the number of reported fans in the United States and the increasing number of television viewers. The overall popularity of sports is one of the reasons it makes sense to devise a business development strategy that utilizes the topic – particularly when it comes to initiating contact, staying on the radar and setting goals.

Initiating Contact

Generating new business is a key component of any industry. Without new clients or customers it's difficult to maintain or grow your success. On a personal level developing new business contacts keeps you well connected and relevant. How can sports help make the crucial connections? We know that about half of all Americans say they're sports fans. According to the United States Census Bureau there are more than 319 million people in the United States.

Divide that in half and you're looking at about 159 million people. That's a conservative estimate of how many people relate to sports or follow sports. If you can talk sports you have an "in" (or a foot in the door) with at least 159 million people.

When you think about those numbers, the odds are pretty good that the person you want to meet or engage with is a sports fan. This reduces the likelihood you're doing the equivalent of cold calling and hoping that someone will respond.

Here's how it works. Time an initial email or make an introductory phone call around a sporting event that could be of interest to your new contact. For example, say you want to reach out to a potential client in Phoenix, Arizona. That city happens to be the site of Super Bowl XLIX on February 1, 2015. You might include something like this in an email. "Your company has been on my radar for a while, and I thought of you with all the talk of Super Bowl preparations. What do you think about the big game being played so close to you?" Close the email with your business "ask."

You can also use big wins as a way to time a congratulatory email. This is the exact approach I use when reaching out to new business contacts. During the football season, I typically send two or three emails on Monday morning based on the people I'm trying to meet and the outcome from Sunday's game.

This approach does a couple of things for me personally. It gives me a schedule to follow when cultivating new contacts and it leads to responses. I get a response about 98 percent of the time and that's an important first step in starting the dialogue and establishing a relationship.

Staying on the Radar

Business doesn't get done after one exchange. You need to nurture relationships and stay on the radar of your contacts or clients. Sports seasons create a number of opportunities to do that naturally.

As I mentioned earlier, the first seven years of my broadcasting career were spent as a producer in Seattle, WA. I was in charge of selecting and writing the stories for the nightly sportscasts. Every December, I mapped out an editorial calendar for the following year. The calendar was based on overall popularity and demand. It included items of local and national interest. That calendar gave me a starting point and served as a reminder of specific games and events that I needed to include in my sportscasts. At a glance, I was able to determine when I should start looking ahead to the college football season, or when I needed to allot time for a major tennis tournament. It was hugely important in staying organized and being productive.

I no longer produce nightly sportscasts, but I still

make an editorial calendar in December and use major sports stories and events as a way to cultivate and maintain business relationships. How does it work?

Let's consider a Major League Baseball season:

- Spring Training starts in February.

- The regular season starts in late March or April and includes 162 games for each team.

- There is an All-Star Game (with the All-Star break) in the middle of the season.

- Post-season games begin at the end of September and run through October.

In addition, there's a good chance each team will go on at least one significant winning and losing streak during the course of the season. That means if you have a baseball-loving client or a contact that lives in a baseball city there are multiple chances to send a note about his or her team throughout the year. The ongoing interactions give you a way to stay on the radar without having to manufacture a reason to reach out and give you something other than work to talk about.

Goal-Setting Device
Sports schedules provide great opportunities for start and stop dates. If you're a sports fan you can use your favorite team to help set deadlines and track your

progress. For example, a basketball fan might look at the upcoming road trips and make a goal to complete a certification class by the time the Lakers return from a 12-day road trip.

Maybe you're looking at a nine-month timeline to implement a new customer service policy. If you live or work in a city that's passionate about hockey, you could use the hockey season as a timeline to mark the beginning, middle and end of your implementation strategy. The opening night of the hockey season kicks off your strategy. The All-Star game marks the halfway point in the season and gives you a chance to evaluate your progress. The start of the playoffs offers a reminder that you're closing in on your deadline and the end of the season marks your completion date.

Here's another example and way to engage your employees in using sports as a goal-setting tool. Consider the time frame for major tennis tournaments. Each Grand Slam event (U.S. Open, Wimbledon, French Open and Australian Open) lasts about two weeks. Is there a two-week goal you can set for your team, or for you personally? The messaging could be something like, "The French Open starts tomorrow. These world-class athletes are going to compete for the next two weeks and so are we. Our goal is to make an additional five sales calls a day until the end of the tournament." The focus here isn't on the sport itself, but the goal you put in place. The added benefit is the opportunity for colleagues to build better relationships through reaching the goal and monitoring the results of the tennis tournament.

Fandom on Display

Leveraging fandom isn't just about you reaching out to other fans. Your fandom is important too. Showing your true colors, or should we say your team colors, draws other fans to you. Giving them a clear idea of your interests gives them a chance to initiate conversations and establish a better connection with you.

Here are ways to bring the conversation to you:

Team Colors. Most corporate environments require professional attire, so wearing a jersey to work is out. But what about incorporating some of your team colors into your wardrobe? How about a red shirt if you're a fan of the Los Angeles Angels of Anaheim, St. Louis Cardinals, or the Arizona Cardinals? Maybe a little green if you're a Boston Celtics or New York Jets fan would work. It's easy for fans in those cities to make the connection and make a comment. In addition, if someone comments on the color of your green shirt it gives you an opening to say, it's in honor of the big Celtics win the night before and begin a conversation.

Team Gear. If you work in a more relaxed environment or your office participates in casual Fridays, then wear your gear. Use your best judgment as to whether a collared shirt with the team logo is more appropriate than a jersey with face paint. Pay attention to colleagues and co-workers who are wearing their jerseys and team gear. A common rooting interest is one of the ways to build camaraderie.

Signing Off. Seahawks quarterback Russell Wilson ends every press conference with the words "Go Hawks!" You can do the same thing in your emails if it doesn't interfere with company policy. Seahawks fans can add a quick "Go Hawks!" instead of the usual "Have a good day!" at the end of their emails to establish a connection to the Seahawks. Every team has a motto or a saying that is recognizable to its fan base that can be used to convey your fandom.

Change Your Ringtone. Try a tune that fans will immediately associate with a team. In Boston it might be "Sweet Caroline" because it prompts a fan sing-along when played in the eighth inning at Red Sox games. Any time the phone rings it can start a discussion from either a fan that recognizes the association with a team or by someone asking why you would choose that particular ring tone.

Carry a Sports Page. I know it sounds old fashioned, but think of a sports page as a subtle accessory that fits under your arm. If you're carrying it with you, keep the picture side out so that everyone can see the stories you're reading up on. After you've finished reading the newspaper, leave the sports page on top so that it draws attention to what you've been reading. (I do this regularly when I travel.) Doing that signals that you're a fan and you're interested in the most relevant story lines.

Quote Machine. Inspirational quotes seem to be as much a part of the game as the Xs and Os. Find a favorite. Print it out and make it visible at your desk. Make sure you attribute the quote to a specific athlete or coach to emphasize your interest in sports.

Pick a Product. In the weeks leading up to the start of the 2014 NFL season, it wasn't uncommon to walk into a Seattle-area grocery store and find a large Skittles display near the registers. Seahawks fans know that the rainbow-colored pellets are the favorite candy of Seattle running back Marshawn Lynch. For a Seahawks fan, keeping a bowl of Skittles on their desk at work is a way to show an interest in their team and strike up conversations throughout the day. Is there a product in your region that conveys a similar message?

Effective Networking

Anyone in business knows that networking is crucial for success. Whether you're trying to get a new job, prospecting new clients, expanding your circle of contacts or looking to increase your influence – all of it happens through networking.

Networking opportunities happen every day. How well are you taking advantage of them? Probably not as well as you think if you're following the old "tried and true" method of handing out business cards and preparing an elevator pitch. Sports fandom and sports conversations give you the upper hand in building relationships that lead to business.

Let me show you how to use sports to become more effective at three main components of networking by slightly tweaking your approach:

1. Opening Question

Without Sports: "Where are you from?"

With Sports: "Who's your team?" or "Which team do you cheer for?"

Here's why – you'll get more information out of asking about a favorite team because more information leads to stronger connections.

For example, I cheer for the Houston Astros because I grew up in Houston. My parents, brother and sister-in-law still live in the Houston area. Even though I've lived in Seattle 15 years I still consider myself a Texas gal and make it home a couple times a year thanks to my job with the Seattle Mariners.

That three-sentence explanation is a treasure trove of information for people looking to connect with me. If you asked me where I'm from the answer is much shorter and would sound something like this. "I grew up in Texas, but live in Seattle." Which answer would you rather have?

Even non-sports fans will give you an explanation as to why they're not interested in sports, which is helpful information for future conversations.

2. The Pitch

Without Sports: Preparing a 30-second pitch relating to what you do.

With Sports: Preparing a 15-second success statement tied to a sports topic.

Here's why – you have limited time to make a good first impression. It's not about you, it's about the person you're trying to connect with or serve. Just because you're talking doesn't mean the other person is listening. You need to have a hook to the conversation.

For example, if you're a Seahawks fan, build on the Super Bowl win. It could sound something like this. "As a Seahawks fan I'm going to be celebrating that Super Bowl win for a long time, but I'm also celebrating the new program we just launched. Both have been huge milestones this year."

That pitch has more intrigue. If the person is interested in hearing more, they'll ask about your program. If they're not interested they have the opportunity to talk about the Seahawks and the Super Bowl.

If the conversation ends up swinging toward the Super Bowl, it doesn't mean you missed your chance to network or make an impression. The conversation is more important than your pitch. People do business when there's a likability and trust factor in place. Conversations get you to that point.

3. Follow up

Without Sports: Forcing business cards or resumes on new contacts.

With Sports: Use the sports calendar to plan follow up conversations.

Here's why – you're not going to get hired or do business after one conversation. Don't force the issue. Look for ways to naturally build relationships over a series of exchanges.

I see this happen all the time. We've been taught to hand out business cards and resumes because somewhere, someone told us you've got to take advantage of your one chance. You do. But it has nothing to do with forcing a resume on someone. I've spent years working alongside professional athletes and coaches. I can tell you from personal experience that it takes an average of five connection points to build the trust I need to effectively work with them. It's not that much different in other work environments.

If you want to build relationships with potential employers or clients, plan out a minimum of five interactions with each person (it's best to use a combination of email, phone and in-person conversations) related to upcoming sporting events or sports headlines.

Chapter Recap

Thinking of sports as a business development tool helps open doors. Use these key takeaways to build business:

Business relationships require interaction and trust

Understand ways you can show your fandom

Initiate contact using a specific sports event

Leverage the sports seasons in follow up conversations

Develop timelines and deadlines based on sports schedules

"Sports fandom and sports conversations give you the upper hand in building relationships that lead to business."

Chapter 7– Conversation Game Plan

"Every conversation has the potential for success and failure."

"Hello! What can I help you find today?"

Chances are if you've ever shopped at Nordstrom you've heard something like this from a sales associate. I myself have heard it many times, although I didn't really notice it until John Nordstrom brought it to my attention. He and I were having breakfast as he corrected and proofread Chapter 1 of this book and the conversation turned to the dialogue sales associates were trained to use.

He explained that most customers were shopping for a specific item so it made sense to ask what it was they were looking for instead of posing a question like: "How are you?"

It's simple and it's brilliant. According to John one of the biggest challenges in making a sale is breaking customer resistance, and you could do that by "genuinely busting your butt" to find what they want. For John's employees asking a question like "How are you today?" didn't get them closer to that goal. Asking about a specific item a customer was looking for did.

It's a great example of how a conversation strategy produces results – not to mention serving as a reminder that short conversations can be powerful. Giving thought to the desired outcome should make a difference in how you approach interactions.

Every conversation has the potential for success and failure. When it comes to sports conversations here are a few things to consider and incorporate into a conversation strategy:

Start Strong. Getting off on the right foot involves knowing whom you're talking to in the first place. You wouldn't walk up to a 3rd grader and ask her how the markets are doing. In the same way, you wouldn't ask about a football game during the middle of June when it's baseball season. You also wouldn't ask an avid golfer and PGA fan which NASCAR driver he follows. If you're not sure what sport to use to start the conversation, ask a question like, "Did you see the game last night?" or "Did you see the end of that tournament?"

This does a couple things: it puts you in the driver's seat and uses a versatile subject. You don't necessarily care whether she did or didn't watch the game or whether he saw the end of the tournament. You just need a place to start. It doesn't matter what answer is given, "yes" or "no" works equally well.

The Art of the Follow up. After you've started the conversation use your question words (Who, What, When, Where, Why, How) to formulate follow up questions.

"What did you think of the game?"
"How about that finish?"

This allows you to gain more insight, further the connection and allows a sports fan to talk about his or her passion. There are plenty of questions to ask related to a sporting event without actually talking about the outcome, so don't limit yourself. For example, a game played at historic Wrigley Field in Chicago could lead to a question like: "Looks like a great ballpark, have you ever been?" Suddenly the conversation could become one about the city of Chicago, favorite places to visit, or an upcoming business trip.

Keep Your Options Open. As a sports reporter, I never know how my interviews or conversations with athletes will end. I only know how it will start. People ask all the time where I get my questions and wonder if someone tells me what to say in my ear. On occasion, I'll be asked to reference a highlight from the game so they can show it while I'm talking to a player, but I am the one responsible for coming up with the questions and asking them. And the questions I come up with are out of curiosity. I'm asking the questions that I want to know the answers to as a fan.

Use that same concept when engaging with your colleagues. Be curious. Even if your co-worker's fly-fishing hobby doesn't interest you, ask the questions that come to mind. Remember this goes back to Chapter 3 and the importance of adding value to your co-worker.

Avoid Assumptions. This is good advice in almost any situation, but be aware of how assumptions impact the way you use sports in conversations. How many times do you assume the woman sitting next to you isn't fan, or assume that 'all' men follow sports?

I remember going to dinner with my husband following the Seahawks NFC Wild Card win over the New Orleans Saints in January 2011. It was a huge upset—win for Seattle. Seahawks running back Marshawn Lynch (nicknamed "Beast Mode") dominated the highlights thanks to a 67—yard run that generated such a cheer from the crowd that a nearby seismic monitoring station registered a small tremor at the stadium. That play became known as the "Beast Quake" and I was on the sidelines for all of it. I was in the locker room getting reactions to the run and to the win.

We ate dinner at the bar and the bartender saw us watching highlights of the game. He looked at my husband and asked what he thought of the game and the run. What the bartender didn't know is that my husband hadn't watched the whole game because he assumed the Seahawks would lose. Several times throughout dinner, the bartender made comments about the game and tried to engage my husband in conversation. When I attempted to jump in, the bartender switched conversation topics and walked away. I was the only person in the restaurant who was on the sidelines for that play and in the locker room after the game, but he assumed I was a woman who didn't watch sports. He assumed wrong. Had he engaged both of us in the conversation he would have received a bigger tip.

Assumptions can cost you, as well as limit both your conversation and business opportunities.

Don't Be Afraid of "No." There is a tendency to be afraid of the word "no." For example, say you ask your co-worker if she saw the game last night. And the only thing she says is, "No."

It can be an intimidating response if you're not prepared, or if you're interviewing a professional athlete on live TV. I've asked questions like, "On that home run, was that the same pitch you fouled off earlier in the at-bat?" Sometimes the answer is "No, that was a different one." A natural response for me in that situation is to ask a follow up on what type of pitch it was.

You can do the same thing if you hear the word "no." Go right back to your question words and try something like, "What were you up to last night?" The follow up opens the door for her to say, "I was working until about 8 o'clock last night. There's so much going on these days." Or "I went to my daughter's choir concert at school." There are lots of different pieces of information you can gather if you can keep the conversation going. Sports got you into the conversation because you probably didn't know to ask about her daughter's concert. You can now file that information away and use it in a future conversation.

Utilizing What You Don't Know. What happens when the conversation turns to you and you don't have any answers? Try putting the unknowns to work for you and realize that what you don't know is as important and helpful as what you do know. You can see this in action during a breaking news scenario.

On June 2, 2010, I headed to Safeco Field, for what I expected to be my normal game–day routine. It was a Wednesday and the Seattle Mariners were playing the Minnesota Twins. I went into the Mariners clubhouse with the rest of the media to begin setting up my interviews for the day and realized this wasn't just any other day. Ken Griffey Jr. wasn't there. For years he had told several media members that when he retired there wouldn't be any fanfare or farewell tours, "One day," he would tell us, "You're going to come into the clubhouse and there's just going to be a sign over my locker that says, 'He gone.'" There was no sign on his locker that June afternoon, but as the day wore on it became clearer and clearer that Griffey was, in fact, gone.

Ken Griffey Jr. was one of the best baseball players in the history of the game, and one of the most beloved sports figures in Seattle. This was breaking news. All the stations in town scrambled to get the information together.

There wasn't much to work with at first. All we knew was that Griffey wasn't at Safeco Field. We didn't know where he was or if he had officially retired. We didn't know if, or when, he was coming back to Seattle. We didn't know what led him to make this decision.

At that point, we did know about Griffey's place among baseball greats. Our producers started building graphics on Griffey's career numbers and scripts were written about the biggest moments in Griffey's career. I started interviewing his Mariner teammates on what they knew and how they were handling the situation.

By the time we went on the air for our pre-game show that night we had received confirmation that Griffey was retiring from baseball, but we still didn't know the reason for the mid-season announcement, what his plans were for the rest of the year, when he would be returning to Seattle, and if he was going to talk to the media. All of those unknowns became talking points during our pregame show that evening. We didn't have the answers but it didn't make the questions any less relevant to the discussion.

I know from personal experience that it can be nerve-wracking to come up with useful information on the spot when you feel like you don't have any to share.

During those moments I take a quick inventory of what I know and what I don't know. Doing that doubles the amount of information I can share with an audience.

When you are able to do that, it allows you to better position yourself as a good conversationalist and as someone who's easy to talk to. For example, let's say you're part of a conversation that revolves around two unbeaten college teams playing in a big conference showdown on Saturday. You don't follow either team closely. Here's a quick list of knowns and unknowns:

- You don't know how their style of play matches up.

- You do know a battle of unbeaten teams is a big deal.

- You do know kickoff is scheduled for 3 o'clock Saturday.

- You don't know if you'll be home to watch it.

Someone has just turned the conversation to you and asked what you think about the game. Here's what that information could look like in a brief 15-second exchange.

"I don't follow either team very closely, so I'm not sure how they'll matchup. But I do know it's a big deal and there will be lots of people watching it Saturday afternoon. I've got a family event to attend and don't know if I'll be home in time to watch it."

There's nothing wrong with that response in the context of a small talk conversation. The game was addressed and a new conversation topic was introduced that can give you something else to talk about.

Define Your Area of Expertise. This is one of the exit strategies I use and encourage others to use when you find yourself in a potentially awkward conversation. There's a common misconception that sports broadcasters know everything there is to know about all sports from the beginning of time up to the present. I can assure you this is not the case. Sports broadcasters are well versed in a number of things, but each one has a specialty or an area of expertise. There are times in a conversation when I could be asked to talk about something outside that realm and I need a gracious way to communicate that, or steer the conversation toward something I'm more comfortable with.

For example, if a basketball fan asks me how I think today's NBA play compares to the NBA in the 1970s, I'm at a total loss. I was born in 1978 and have no memory of professional basketball before the mid 1980's. That's when I started watching basketball on television with my dad and attending basketball games with my family.

Here's how I could frame a response to a question about basketball in the 1970s, "You know I didn't really start watching the NBA until the mid '80s. I loved watching the Lakers on TV with my dad and it's how I ended up playing basketball through high school. These days I follow more football than basketball."

It's a 15-second response that opens the door to multiple conversation topics like the NBA in the 1980s, the LA Lakers, my family and my high school basketball career. In addition, it draws a bull's-eye around a topic that I would consider my area of expertise, football.

This approach works in a lot of ways. And "expertise" in this situation doesn't mean you have to direct people to something you could talk about for hours at a time. Remember, this is most likely part of a short small talk discussion leading up to a business conversation.

Consider the following statements and see if you can identify the area of expertise:

- "I'm not much of a golfer. I don't seem to have the patience, but I do love spending time hiking on the weekends."[4]

- "I'm a football fan, but just started following the Cowboys closely when I moved to Dallas a few months ago."[5]

- "I didn't watch sports much until recently when I took a new sales position and wanted a way to connect with my clients."[6]

- "It was such a busy morning, I only had time to read the sports headlines on my way out the door. I haven't had time to read the full stories."[7]

Defining your area of expertise works when talking sports or just about anything else. Let's say you were asked for a restaurant recommendation on the opposite side of town. How about this response: "I don't know that area very well, but I can give you a couple great places just south of there."

No, but... This is the second type of exit strategy I recommend and it's designed to convey honesty and encourage the conversation to continue. If someone

---

[4] Expertise: hiking

[5] Expertise: general football story lines

[6] Expertise: recent sports headlines

[7] Expertise: today's headlines

strikes up a conversation with you using the game from last night and you didn't watch the game do not lie and say you did. It's bad form to lie in business and it's a recipe for disaster when the follow up questions start and you get caught in the lie. Instead you're going to be honest and respond by saying something like:

"No, but what happened?"

"No, but who won?"

"No, but was it a good game?"

Any of these responses, and many more, will work to keep you out of a potentially sticky situation and asking a follow up question of your own will keep the conversation alive and give you information about the game you didn't watch that you can use later on.

Additional Conversation Strategies

All of these techniques help increase your ability and confidence to use sports topics in business conversations. They're also helping you become a better overall conversationalist and a more effective communicator. The best communicators are equally aware of their surroundings and audience as they are of the actual words they're saying, which is why you should consider using these strategies as well.

Set Expectations. Everyone dreads conversations that drag on too long. Some people don't have a good sense of time, and others don't realize the time constraints you might be under. If you have conversation expectations it's best to lay them out so that both of you get on the same page. This is exactly what I do with players right before and even during an interview.

Before the interview I'll say, "We only have about two minutes so I'm going to ask you about three questions." During the interview I might say "I'm going to come back to the offense as a whole in a minute, but I want to ask what you saw on that play at third base." By saying, "I'm going to come back to that in a minute" I'm giving the player a heads up as to what's coming next. As I start the final question, I might use a word like "lastly" or "finally" to indicate we're nearing the end of the interview.

You could apply a similar approach and set your expectations in a variety of ways. Here is an example: "I've only got a couple minutes, but I wanted to see how your daughter's concert was last night."

When the two minutes are up, you don't look rude for saying, "I've got to run. I'll circle back with you on Friday's meeting later in the week."

You laid out the expectations and are sticking to a timeline. How about this exchange:

"I don't have time for a full rundown on the report, but give me your best summary in four sentences before I head into my next meeting."

Giving specific directions sends a clear message as to what you're looking for and how the other person should respond.

If, despite your best efforts, the conversation continues longer than you want or have time for, offer a way to continue the exchange – via email. If it's a work-related conversation, you'll be able to get the pertinent information and follow up when you have a window of time in your schedule. If your co-worker is rambling, however, the act of writing it down in an email will likely alert them to the fact that they weren't on track. Chances are that email never gets sent, saving you from further discussion.

Watch the Clock. Time management issues can create headaches during the course of a business day. Don't add to the problem by underestimating the time you spend talking to your co-workers. If you say something like, "Do you have two minutes? I just have a quick question for you." and then engage in a 20-minute conversation, you run the risk of annoying your co-workers.

I've seen this happen quite a bit with reporters asking for an interview. They'll ask for a quick two- or three-minute interview as a ploy to get the athlete to say yes, then end up doing a 20-minute interview with an athlete who only agreed to talk because he was told it was going to be a couple minutes long. In my experience that's a good way to erode trust and limit your conversation opportunities from ever happening.

If measuring a conversation in minutes seems too difficult, try the technique I use when interviewing professional athletes. I will often ask if they have time to answer three questions. Two of which I've already thought out and the third I use as a follow up to something they've said. At the end of the three questions, I end the interview. They're often surprised and always appreciate that I've kept my word and not wasted their time.

If what I really need is a 15-minute interview, I will set the expectations up front and ask for the time I need. Prior to the interview I will set a timer or watch the clock to make sure I stick within the agreed upon time frame. The athletes appreciate that I'm considerate of their schedules, and because of that, I have much more confidence that when I ask for an interview I will get it.

Using the same techniques will help ensure that you maintain good relationships with your colleagues and have the access you need when you need it.

Pick Up on Cues. The actual words used during a conversation are only part of the communication process. Researchers have determined that up to 93 percent of communication is nonverbal. That means people around you are likely responding to your conversation without saying a word. Are you picking up on their cues? If your colleague is looking at his watch, taking a step toward the door, or becoming distracted with other things...you have worn out your welcome. It's best to wrap up and end the conversation, unless it's an urgent matter that needs immediate attention.

Allow for Outside Influences. This is a nicer way of saying "It's not all about you." There are times when awkward conversations occur because a co-worker is stressed or a client is dealing with a set of challenges. There are a number of outside factors that can influence a conversation that have nothing to do with you. Before you walk away and wonder if it was something that you said, take a minute to review your past exchanges. Are they generally pleasant? Do you have a good relationship with this person? If so, then don't dwell on it and just move on. If you answered "no" to those questions, try the previous strategies to improve your conversations.

Chapter Recap

Make a conversation plan. Use these key takeaways to improve your overall communication:

Prepare for conversations in advance

Lean on exit strategies to avoid awkward situations

Avoid assumptions that can limit opportunities

No isn't a word to fear

"The best communicators are equally aware of their surroundings and audience as they are of the actual words they're saying."

Chapter 8 – Guaranteed Success

"The "what ifs" you hear are not related to your competency, but your confidence. Do not let a lack of confidence impact how you or others view your competency."

My business cards say "sports reporter" and "expert talker" but even the expert develops a case of the "what ifs" from time to time. Not familiar with the "what ifs?" It's that internal dialogue that tries to throw you off track. For me it sounds like this:

What if I say the wrong thing?

What if I ask a silly question?

What if they think I'm not smart enough to do the job?

I thought I was able to ignore those questions, until I was called out by former Mariners pitcher Mark Lowe in the middle of the clubhouse. I was trying to ask for an interview to be used in the Mariners pre-game show, but instead of walking up to him and asking for two minutes of his time, I beat around the bush. I stood there and hemmed and hawed for a couple minutes before he finally interrupted.

"What are you doing?" he said in an embarrassingly loud voice. "If you want an interview ask for it. You know us, you know that we'll do it, just ask and stop dancing around it."

I was floored – and slightly embarrassed. But he was right. I'd failed to give him what he needed in the conversation – a short, direct and informative exchange – because I lacked the confidence that he would agree to an interview. My fear of failure led me to soft-pedal the "ask," it was my way of softening the blow if he said, "No."

But he didn't say no. And he wasn't going to say no. He knew I had a job to do and I knew that I had spent a lot of time cultivating the relationships I needed with everyone in the clubhouse, including him. So why didn't I just trust my position and my skills? Because everyone – even the expert talker – experiences a "confidence crisis" at some point.

In those moments, it's important to remember that the "what ifs" you hear are not related to your competency, but your confidence. Do not let a lack of confidence impact how you or others view your competency. Remember the people around you are picking up on your cues just like you are reading theirs. I talk to a number of executives throughout sports as part of my job and for my business. If I approached any of them and asked for a meeting the same way I asked Mark for an interview, I probably wouldn't get the meeting. But even if I did, a timid, beat-around-the-bush approach creates doubt in their minds as to whether I'm capable of doing my job. Conveying confidence in your skills and the way you talk to other people allows them to see your competency.

Everyone needs a confidence boost from time to time. Here are three questions I use to remind myself why I have reasons to be confident around the athletes I cover and with the corporate clients I work with:

1. **Have you done your homework?** Knowing the material you'd like to discuss and being able to identify specific things you want to address will help you stay on track. You're not trying to make a social call. You've got work to do.

2. **Do you have a job to do?** Not speaking up when you have a job to do will cost you valuable time and most likely future opportunities. I had a job to do in the clubhouse and needed to get that interview. Coming up empty handed was not an option in that situation.

3. **Do you have credibility on your side?** It's a lot easier to approach any situation if you have a few successes under your belt along with the respect of your peers. Too many people forget that they're in this position. Flash back to a past conversation or meeting that went well to help banish the "what ifs."

Here's another reason to be confident in the skills you've learned throughout this book: Sports works every single time. I guarantee it.

Prior to the Super Bowl in February 2014, I chimed in on an online discussion about the best small talk topics. You can probably guess that I made a case for sports and used the Super Bowl as an example. A woman responded to my comments by posting this,

"Let me tell you about a time when this didn't work for me. I was at the grocery store and the cashier helping me had orange hair. I asked if he was a Broncos fan and trying to support the team by wearing their team colors. He said he wasn't a football fan at all and explained that it was an unfortunate coloring accident. See, sports doesn't always work."

I can understand her point of view and perhaps her embarrassment, but the woman who wrote this is wrong. Sports worked just fine. If the goal was to strike up a conversation, sports did its job. If sustaining the conversation was her goal, she did not do her job. The cashier didn't have to be a sports fan. If she wanted to continue the conversation she could have asked about the salon he went to or asked why he colored his hair to begin with. The point here is this: failure is measured against the desired outcome. People who try and tell me sports doesn't work can't see how many avenues one sports conversation provides and often didn't know what their conversational goal was to begin with.

That brings us back to John Nordstrom. He knew what his goals were and he knew how important individual conversations were in reaching those goals. It's why the Nordstrom sales associates were trained to ask, "What can I help you find today?" and it's what led to an interesting observation during a

Seahawks practice one winter day during the 2013 season.

I was watching practice and John walked over to me and said, "Jen, there are three things that really impress me about Pete Carroll and this organization. Would you like to know what they are?"

Of course I was all ears. I pulled the pen from my pocket and started taking notes as John continued.

"Number one," he said. "Everyone is included. It's amazing. Everyone feels like they're part of the team from the guys on the practice squad to the training staff and the front office. It's not like that in every organization.

"Number two," he continued. "Is that no one wants to take credit for any of the success. Pete gives credit to John [Schneider]. John gives credit to Pete. They both credit the owner and the staff; it just goes on and on.

"But it's the third thing that impresses me most of all," John said as he leaned in a little closer. "Pete understands the importance of the last three feet."

I stopped writing for a moment and looked at him. I'm pretty sure the look said it all. I had no idea what he was talking about. John sensed this and before he explained he positioned himself three feet in front of me.

"The last three feet is something we talked about with our sales staff because it's the most important and the most difficult space to cover. It's the distance between me and the customer."

Think about your shopping habits. How many times have you carried something around the store, only to decide on your way to the register that you really don't need it and put it back. The last three feet are crucial to making a sale. John related this sales concept to Pete Carroll and the Seahawks in terms of buy-in.

"Watch him," John said. "He gets it. He'll pull guys aside and talk to them one-on-one. He lets them know he cares. He takes the time to figure out their unique skills and puts them in a position to succeed. It's all part of the last three feet."

Less than eight weeks later the Seahawks won the Super Bowl.

Pete and John were both very strategic in their approaches. They understood how personal connections and conversations could close a deal and lead to big wins.

The Most Important Conversation
Think for a moment about the most important conversations of your career. What stands out as the conversation that's made the biggest difference to

date? Are you thinking about the conversation you had when you were hired? Or maybe the one where you learned about a raise or a promotion?

All of those conversations played a role in your success and getting you to where you are today, but they weren't the most important.

One conversation can change the course of your career and your business forever. But it's not the one you think.

Often when we think of the life altering conversations we jump to the moments listed above. Those examples however are the end result of a number of conversations. The most important was the first one. The first time you had a chance to get in front of your potential employer. The first time you met your new client. The first time you had a chance to break the ice, make an introduction and make an impression. That was the most important conversation.

Go back over the conversation you identified as being the most important, and see if you can trace it all the way back to the first encounter. Do you remember what you said? Do you remember what you talked about? Do you remember who was in the room?

A few weeks before I learned about the "last three feet" from John, I made a trip out to Seattle Chocolates to pick up an order of chocolate bars. I had been making regular trips to pick up chocolate for thank you gifts for about a year and a half, but this trip was different. The chocolate bars I loaded into the back of the car that day were mine. I was tearing up as I left the parking lot with my 400 Sports Bars, a special collaboration between the Talk Sporty to Me brand and Seattle Chocolates.

I thought back to how I had gotten to the point of having my chocolate bar and where it all started − on a golf course. That's where I met Jean Thompson, the CEO of Seattle Chocolates, and her executive team. We were playing in a charity tournament, although I'm not sure you could call what I did that day "playing golf." Jean wasn't much of a golfer either and what we lacked in golfing ability we more than made up for in conversation.

By the end of the afternoon, I knew I liked Jean, the company and their products. I left thinking about ways I could support Seattle Chocolates. Doing business with her was the furthest thing from my mind. I started using their chocolate bars as a way to say "thanks" and every couple months I would swing by their offices, pick up more chocolate and chat with whoever was around.

After about a year of doing that, I approached them with the idea of the Sports Bar, about six months later I was driving away from Seattle Chocolates with 400 of them loaded in my car. The Sports Bar is now available online through Seattle Chocolates. It's made a difference in my business as both a revenue stream, and a branding tool.

One conversation can make a huge difference even if it's not apparent at the time. When you think about where one conversation can lead it becomes very clear that your ability to communicate is one of the top predictors of your success.

You've got the smarts, the savvy and the know-how. Make all of your conversations count. It's worth it.

Chapter Recap

Successful conversations can help you rack up big wins in business if you remember these key takeaways:

'What ifs' question your confidence not your competency

Important conversations happen on a daily basis

Never forget the importance of the last three feet

"It takes time to create excellence. If it could be done so quickly, more people would do it."
John Wooden

What Do I Say If...?

"You can communicate all you want, but if [teammates] don't understand what you're saying, you're gonna be in a tough spot."

Earl Thomas
Safety,
Seattle Seahawks

So you've finished this book and you're developing a strategy to put all your conversation tools to use. I'd like to tell you that it's smooth sailing from here on out, but you're bound to run into a couple of obstacles from time to time and even a few sports jerks. Don't get discouraged and don't let one bad or uncomfortable conversation keep you from trying again.

I've identified five situations that I've been asked about most often and done my best to give you a way to respond graciously.

What if I encounter a fan spewing an enormous amount of statistics and expecting me to respond to all the numbers?

Not everyone memorizes large amounts of statistics. If you don't follow the numbers or don't care about the numbers, acknowledge that and turn the conversation toward the topic you're more comfortable talking about. For example: "That's a lot of numbers to follow and to be honest, I don't get into all the stats. I do like the matchup and the way the offense has looked lately."

What if I walk into a client's office and I don't see any indication he or she is a sports fan? Then what do I talk about?

I would still recommend starting with sports. Try asking about either the most popular sport in the city or the sport that's currently in season. Let's say your client is in Cleveland, Ohio. There's an opportunity to ask about a professional baseball, basketball or football team depending on the season, not to mention the popularity of college football in Ohio.

Keep your initial inquiry broad. For example: "How do you think the Cavs are going to do this year?" or "How have the Browns looked this season?"

Remember it doesn't matter if your client follows either of those teams; you're just looking for a way into the conversation that will lead to follow up questions and conversations. If your client says she doesn't watch the Cavs but is a huge baseball fan, shift your line of questioning. If your client scoffs at your inquiry about the Browns and says that he's a Green Bay Packers fan you can ask follow up questions related to the Packers.

What if I get an overwhelming negative response to asking a sports question, like someone who says, "I hate sports. I don't know why anyone would waste their time with it."

First, try not to take offense, especially if you are a passionate sports fan. Second, remember the purpose of your conversation. If you're in a business setting, it's probably best not to argue over the merits of talking sports at work. (Although perhaps you could purchase of a few of these books and hand them out as Christmas presents.) In a business interaction, I recommend turning the conversation to whatever it is the other person wants to talk about by saying something like this:

"On occasion I've wasted time watching sports on the weekends, but I also enjoy getting out and going wine tasting. How about you? What do you do in your free time?"

If you feel comfortable, or you're in a more social setting, you can ask about the negative response to sports. Avoid making accusatory statements or aggressive comments. Stay even-keeled and try something like: "That's a pretty strong response. What is it that you don't like about sports?"

What if I'm having a sports conversation and someone says, "You don't know what you're talking about. I watched the game and you're completely wrong."

Take this response with a grain of salt and resist the urge to either run away or engage in an argument. Sports is mostly objective. Unless you're actually arguing the final score of a game, a specific stat, player name or something along those lines, sports conversations are often based on opinion. Trust me, after a lifetime around sports fans and more than a decade in sports broadcasting I've heard some crazy opinions, but that doesn't make them wrong. Unlikely? Maybe. Off-the-wall? Sometimes. But if it's your opinion stick with it and if it makes you feel more comfortable offer a brief explanation as to why you feel that way. For example:

- "I think the team was really undisciplined last night based on what I saw in the second quarter. Maybe it got better after I turned the game off."

- "I didn't get to watch much of the game, but in the little that I saw the defense looked terrible."

- "You and I have completely different opinions then, because I thought it was a great win considering how many starters were injured."

What if I get asked about a game that I won't be watching or even following?

Utilize your exit strategies listed as part of Chapter 7 and remember that an exit strategy doesn't mean you're exiting the conversation altogether. They were designed to help you leave the awkward part of the conversation. You don't have to watch a game just because someone else is, so be honest about your lack of interest in the game or inability to watch it. For example:

- "I know it's Game 7 tonight, but I didn't get into the World Series this year. I'll count on you to fill me in on what I miss."

- "I've got a client dinner tonight and won't get home until late, so I'm going to miss the game."

Worst Ways to Use Sports at Work

By now you know there are plenty of productive ways to use sports conversations to improve communication skills, build relationships and create business opportunities. But not all sports conversations are created equal. There is a point when fans can become overzealous and do more harm than good when talking about their team or expressing their fandom.

Using sports in these ways can hurt your relationships, decrease your likability and limit your opportunities. Don't become the sports jerk or sports bully in the office. Avoid the following scenarios at work:

Power Play. Unless you work in the sports industry it doesn't matter if you can correctly recite every stat from last night's game. (Let me let you in on a little secret – even when you work in sports we don't memorize every stat – that's what game notes are for.) Your impulse to spout stat after stat to prove how much you know ruins your chance to build rapport. You'd be better off explaining how much you studied the material for the upcoming presentation than trying to prove how smart you are as a fan.

Being a "Know-It-All." This goes hand in hand with the "power play." No one likes a know-it-all, in fact that's one of the top complaints I hear from people who are irritated with their sports-talking co-workers. They're not impressed, and your likeability takes a hit when you spout all of your "knowledge." The goal of sports talk at work is to engage with your co-workers and colleagues. That won't happen if you try to be a know-it-all. Make sure you allow an exchange of ideas during a conversation instead of delivering a one-sided monologue.

Personal Attacks. Passionate fans can feel so closely connected with a team or a player that negative comments about their team can feel like an attack aimed squarely at the heart, soul and even character of the fan. If that's the way your comments are perceived, it will impact your ability to build a relationship. Avoid saying things that could be perceived as an attack. For example:

- "That was such a stupid move. I can't believe anyone would pay money to see a team do that every night."

- "How could anyone think that trade would pay off? They clearly weren't thinking straight on that one."

- "What kind of moron makes that decision with under two minutes to play?"

Picking Fights. One of the reasons sports conversations work is because they keep you away from the hot button topics. Don't turn a great, all-encompassing subject into a fight in the break room. For example, when you choose to focus on a team's off-the-field issues instead of the most recent game, you're ruining a great opportunity to build relationships. In addition, a general tendency to pick fights or be a divisive person at work can limit your opportunities.

Badge of Honor. So you watched every inning of baseball played by your local team and DVR'd every football game to watch three times as "film study." Kudos to you, but no one cares. No one in your office, anyway, who is trying to focus on his or her job in addition to running their kids to soccer, ballet and piano, as well as grocery shopping and getting the house cleaned. There's nothing wrong with being invested in your team, but don't expect everyone else to feel the same way. Certainly don't expect your level of fanaticism to raise your status at work. Your "film study" is a conversation to be had on sports radio or during a pre-game tailgate, but not at the office.

"There are plenty of productive ways to use sports conversations to improve communication skills, build relationships and create business opportunities. But not all sports conversations are created equal"

Quick Guide to Networking with Sports

"The separation is in the preparation."

Russell Wilson
Quarterback,
Seattle Seahawks

Break out of the rut and really capture someone's attention.

It's important because research has shown attention spans are shrinking. According to Harvard Business School history professor Nancy Koehn, in 2013 the average attention span of Americans was about eight seconds. By comparison goldfish have an attention span of nine seconds.

Knowing that you've got to capture someone's attention in a hurry to keep him or her focused on what you have to say, using the same old script won't cut it. We covered this in Chapter 6, but here's a quick guide to effective networking using sports:

Use the Background Noise. Are you at a function being held at a restaurant or bar? There's likely to be at least one television turned to a game or a sports channel. Use the game as a starting point or make a reference to one of the top stories of the day. Then bring the conversation around to a topic you're comfortable talking about. For example:

- "I see they've got the Bruins–Flyers game on. Hockey for me is a way to pass the time until the Patriots play again on Sunday. How about you?"

- "Every time I look up at the TV, they're talking about Carson Palmer. His injury must be pretty bad, but I didn't watch the game. Have you seen the highlights?"

Look For Other Clues. If you're not in a venue with a television, look for other clues like someone who might be wearing the logo of a specific team, or signage around the venue supporting a local team or an upcoming viewing party.

Jump Right In. If you're still not finding a sports giveaway, jump into the conversation with a sports topic anyway. Use a topic relating to a local team or a national headline. Remember more than half of all Americans are sports fans and you don't care about the sports as much as the opportunity to get to know someone.

Collect Data. Are you talking to a baseball fan, a soccer dad, a football junkie? Make sure you take note of the team or sport they follow. If you're talking to a non–sports fan identify at least one hobby that could be used in future conversations.

Transition to Business. It's as simple as saying something like, "When you're not watching football, what do you do?"

Respond Briefly. When the question comes back to you and your line of work, keep it short. Just one or two sentences or better yet, think back to our 15–second conversations. If the person you're talking to is interested he or she will ask for more details.

Plan a Follow up. If business cards are exchanged, do more than promise an email the next day. Verbalize a specific plan to follow up relating to the information you gathered during the conversation. For example:

- "I'll email you after the Patriots win this weekend."

- "I'll get back to you before you get too involved in planning your next hiking trip."

Follow Through. Don't get sidetracked or forget to actually send the follow up email. The person you met could be your next biggest client, your next best employee or a valued business connection.

"Yeah"

Marshawn Lynch
Running Back,
Seattle Seahawks

Epilogue

"Studies show people who talk more are happier. Go ahead be happy."

This is just the beginning of the conversations for you. My hope is that you use the information in this book to spark more productive conversations with your colleagues, clients and business contacts.

To extend the conversation to an even larger group, I encourage you to consider Talk Sporty to Me: Thinking Outside the Box Scores as your next book club selection and **download the discussion questions** on the website at TalkSportyToMe.com. Bulk orders are eligible for a discount. For more information contact Norsemen Books: info@norsemenbooks.com or 1-206-734-4950

For additional information on how to build your sports knowledge base I recommend purchasing my first book, **Game Time: Learn to Talk Sports in 5 Minutes a Day for Business.** I wrote that to be the go-to guide for new and novice sports fans and it details how to use limited sports knowledge in conversations at work. It also helps determine where to start your sports fandom, which brings me to this final note.

As you might have noticed, many of the sports examples used in the book relate to football and the NFL. I have been asked why and if I purposely stayed away from sports like hockey and soccer. The answer is "yes" and "no." I was very intentional in using the NFL-based examples for two reasons, the most obvious being my employment by the Seattle Seahawks. The bigger reason I chose football examples so often throughout the book is because of the overall popularly of the sport. Research has shown that football is the most popular sport among American sports fans and of those fans, more watch the NFL than college football.

Football is certainly not the only sport to use in conversations at work, but it's a good place to start – especially if you're a new or novice fan looking for the greatest reach in your conversations.

Finally, I know you can do it.

You can use sports conversations to generate business, advance your career and gain access to key influencers.

I want to help you celebrate those successes. Send me an email at: Jen@TalkSportyToMe.com and I'll cheer you on because I know it's "game on" for you.

About the Author

"Every job is a self - portrait of the person who did it. Autograph your work with excellence."

Jen Mueller, America's Expert Talker, pursued a career in sports broadcasting after repeated comments of "talks too much" from teachers and family members. Jen is a lifelong sports fan and a veteran sports broadcaster.

A former high school athlete, Jen turned her attention to officiating in college. She made her mark first as an intramural flag-football official and earned All-American honors as one of the best officials in the United States. She transitioned to officiating tackle football and spent 10 years on the sidelines of high school games. Her officiating experience helped prepare her for her current role as the radio sideline reporter for the Seattle Seahawks. She is the proud owner of a Super Bowl ring for her work on the broadcast team.

In addition to her NFL experience, Jen is a college sideline reporter for ROOT SPORTS and is part of the Mariners television broadcast team. In 2012, she was the first person to interview Felix Hernandez after he threw the first perfect game in Mariners franchise history. In addition to her on-air work, Jen is an Emmy-nominated producer for her work on Mariners All Access.

Jen launched Talk Sporty to Me in 2009 after identifying a communication void that could be filled with sports conversations. She works with corporate clients on how to find value in being a sports fan in business. Her past clients include the Seattle Seahawks, Seattle Mariners, T-Mobile, Coca-Cola, Community Bankers of Washington, and the Accounting & Financial Women's Alliance. Jen is a talented and dynamic speaker with unique content and personal stories from inside professional locker rooms. She is also the author of Game Time: Learn to Talk Sports in 5 Minutes a Day for Business published in May of 2013.

Jen graduated from Southern Methodist University in 2000 with degrees in broadcasting journalism and public policy. She currently lives in the Seattle area.

To book Jen to speak at your conference or event, please email: Jen@TalkSportyToMe.com or call 1-866-202-9718